EDUCATION IN A COMPETITIVE AND GLOBALIZING WORLD

COLLEGE CREDIT AND DEBIT CARDS

TRENDS, ISSUES, ANALYSES

EDUCATION IN A COMPETITIVE AND GLOBALIZING WORLD

Additional books in this series can be found on Nova's website under the Series tab.

Additional e-books in this series can be found on Nova's website under the e-book tab.

EDUCATION IN A COMPETITIVE AND GLOBALIZING WORLD

COLLEGE CREDIT AND DEBIT CARDS

TRENDS, ISSUES, ANALYSES

EVALYN LINETTE TRENT
EDITOR

NOVINKA
New York

For permission to use material from this book please contact us:
Telephone 631-231-7269; Fax 631-231-8175
Web Site: http://www.novapublishers.com

Library of Congress Cataloging-in-Publication Data

ISBN: 978-1-63321-116-2

Published by Nova Science Publishers, Inc. † New York

CONTENTS

PREFACE

This book examines trends associated with and characteristics of college affinity card agreements; the extent of marketing for college affinity cards and college student credit cards; what is known about the effect of use of these cards on student credit card debt; the functions of college cards and the characteristics of schools and card providers offering the cards; and benefits and concerns regarding these cards.

Chapter 1 – Institutions of higher education, alumni groups, and other affiliated organizations may enter into agreements with credit card issuers for "college affinity cards," in which issuers use the institution's name or logo in exchange for payments. Separately, some credit card issuers offer "college student credit cards," which are expressly targeted to students. Partly in response to concerns about card issuer practices and rising student credit card debt, Congress passed the Credit Card Accountability Responsibility and Disclosure Act of 2009. The act includes consumer protections and requires disclosures specifically for consumers under the age of 21, including limits to on-campus credit card marketing and requirements for public disclosure of affinity card agreements. The act mandates that GAO review these agreements and assess their effect on student credit card debt.

This chapter examines (1) trends associated with and characteristics of college affinity card agreements, (2) the extent of marketing for college affinity cards and college student credit cards, and (3) what is known about the effect of use of these cards on student credit card debt. GAO analyzed data from the Federal Reserve and CFPB, including a sample of 39 affinity agreements filed by the issuers. GAO also analyzed data on student credit card use or indebtedness, and interviewed officials from federal agencies, credit card issuers, and affiliated organizations.

Chapter 2 – A growing number of colleges and universities have entered into agreements with financial firms to provide debit and prepaid card services for students. As the number of agreements has grown, questions have arisen over fees and issues such as student choice. This chapter examines (1) the functions of college cards and the characteristics of schools and card providers offering the cards; and (2) benefits and concerns regarding these cards. GAO reviewed relevant federal laws and regulations, developed a tally of card agreements by reviewing industry reports and school and provider websites, and analyzed data and interviewed officials from federal agencies, banks and other financial firms, students, and industry and consumer groups. GAO selected nine schools (which vary by program length and sector) for extended interviews and data collection.

In: College Credit and Debit Cards
Editor: Evalyn Linette Trent
ISBN: 978-1-63321-116-2

Chapter 1

CREDIT CARDS: MARKETING TO COLLEGE STUDENTS APPEARS TO HAVE DECLINED*

United States Government Accountability Office

WHY GAO DID THIS STUDY

Institutions of higher education, alumni groups, and other affiliated organizations may enter into agreements with credit card issuers for "college affinity cards," in which issuers use the institution's name or logo in exchange for payments. Separately, some credit card issuers offer "college student credit cards," which are expressly targeted to students. Partly in response to concerns about card issuer practices and rising student credit card debt, Congress passed the Credit Card Accountability Responsibility and Disclosure Act of 2009. The act includes consumer protections and requires disclosures specifically for consumers under the age of 21, including limits to on-campus credit card marketing and requirements for public disclosure of affinity card agreements. The act mandates that GAO review these agreements and assess their effect on student credit card debt.

This chapter examines (1) trends associated with and characteristics of college affinity card agreements, (2) the extent of marketing for college affinity cards and college student credit cards, and (3) what is known about the effect of use of these cards on student credit card debt. GAO analyzed data

* This is an edited, reformatted and augmented version of United States Government Accountability Office Publication, No. GAO-14-225, dated February 2014.

from the Federal Reserve and CFPB, including a sample of 39 affinity agreements filed by the issuers. GAO also analyzed data on student credit card use or indebtedness, and interviewed officials from federal agencies, credit card issuers, and affiliated organizations.

What GAO Recommends

GAO makes no recommendations in this report.

What GAO Found

Trends associated with college affinity card agreements include fewer agreements and cardholders and declining payments, according to data GAO analyzed from the Board of Governors of the Federal Reserve System (Federal Reserve) and the Bureau of Consumer Financial Protection (CFPB). The number of affinity card agreements declined from 1,045 in 2009 to 617 in 2012 (41 percent). More than 70 percent of the agreements in 2012 were with institutions of higher education or alumni organizations, and one issuer—FIA Card Services, a subsidiary of Bank of America—had 67 percent of all agreements. Affinity card issuers paid $50.4 million to all organizations in 2012, 40 percent less than in 2009. In most cases, payments were based on numbers of cardholders and the amount spent on the cards. The card agreements covered contractual obligations related to such things as marketing practices, target populations, use of the organization's logo or trademark, terms of payment, and, in some cases, service standards.

Student-focused marketing of affinity and student cards on campus appears to have declined. Four large affinity card issuers GAO interviewed (representing 91 percent of cardholders) said that they primarily targeted alumni and no longer marketed affinity cards directly to students. In interviews with GAO, institutions of higher education and affiliated organizations agreed that affinity card marketing directly to students had ceased. In addition, five of the nine largest overall credit card issuers that also issue college student credit cards told GAO they no longer actively marketed these cards (such as through direct mail, e-mail, or on-campus activity), but rather relied upon websites and bank branches. Representatives of five institutions with large affinity card agreements told GAO that they generally noticed a decline in on-campus credit card marketing in recent years. Consistent with these observations, available data show a decline in card solicitations to students in recent years. For example, a survey of students in 2013 by Student Monitor, a research firm, found that 6 percent of students reported obtaining a credit card as a result of a direct mail solicitation, compared with 36 percent in 2000.

Data are not available to definitively determine the effect that affinity cards and college student credit cards have had on student credit card debt. For affinity cards, the effect may be limited because fewer students appear to hold such cards. For college student credit cards, the effect is difficult to determine because data are available for credit cards in general but not for student credit cards in particular. However, students' overall use of credit cards appears to have declined in recent years. For example, Student Monitor reported 33 percent of students owned credit cards in 2013 versus 53 percent in 2004, a trend corroborated by several other studies that GAO identified. But Student Monitor found that students with credit cards in their names increasingly obtained the cards before starting college. In addition, it found that in 2013, students charged an average of $171 monthly on their cards, 80 percent of the cards had a credit limit of $1,000 or less, and 72 percent of students said they paid their outstanding charges in full each month. Student Monitor also reported that one quarter of students in 2013 paid a late payment fee at least once since they acquired the credit card, with almost half of those paying more than once.

Abbreviations

CFPB	Bureau of Consumer Financial Protection
DCI	data collection instrument

February 25, 2014

The Honorable Tim Johnson
Chairman

The Honorable Mike Crapo
Ranking Member
Committee on Banking, Housing, and Urban Affairs
United States Senate
The Honorable Jeb Hensarling

Chairman

The Honorable Maxine Waters
Ranking Member
Committee on Financial Services
House of Representatives

Institutions of higher education and affiliated organizations, such as alumni associations, sometimes have agreements with credit card issuers for "college affinity cards." These cards often bear the name or logo of the school or organization, and, in return, the issuer pays a portion of the proceeds of the credit card to the school or organization. In addition, some card issuers offer "college student credit cards" that are unaffiliated with a particular institution but designed specifically for college students. Consumer advocates and some members of Congress have had concerns in recent years about student credit card debt and the marketing practices, such as on-campus solicitations, used to enroll students in cards.[1]

To address some of these concerns, Congress passed the Credit Card Accountability Responsibility and Disclosure Act of 2009 (CARD Act).[2] Among other things, the act requires card issuers to file annually with federal regulators the terms and conditions of their college affinity credit card agreements with institutions of higher education or affiliated organizations.[3] The CARD Act also mandates that we report on several issues related to college affinity and college student credit cards.[4] This report examines (1) the trends associated with and characteristics of college affinity card agreements, (2) the extent of marketing for college affinity and college student credit cards, and (3) what is known about the effect of the use of affinity cards and student credit cards on student credit card debt.

To address our first objective, we reviewed annual reports submitted to Congress by the Board of Governors of the Federal Reserve System (Federal Reserve) and the Bureau of Consumer Financial Protection, also known as the Consumer Financial Protection Bureau (CFPB), and analyzed the public database of agreements that are reported by issuers annually to them. We assessed the reliability of these databases by interviewing Federal Reserve and CFPB officials knowledgeable about the data and checking the data for illogical values or obvious errors. We found the data to be sufficiently reliable for describing the general characteristics and trends of the affinity card marketplace. For in-depth analysis, we further selected a subset of active agreements using a nonprobability sample of 39 college affinity card agreements between issuers and institutions of higher education or affiliated organizations from 2011 (the most recent year for which the agreements were available). 5 The sample included the agreements with the largest number of cardholders overall, for each issuer, and for institutions of higher education. Collectively, the agreements in our sample covered about 38 percent of all cardholders associated with affinity credit cards in 2011, which allows us to make statements of context and describe multiple factors relating to college credit card agreements. Findings from this limited review cannot be generalized to the overall population of all agreements for college affinity cards in 2011. We also interviewed representatives of six institutions of higher education and affiliated organizations, including those party to three of the four largest agreements, as determined by number of cardholders. For the second and third objectives, we reviewed studies, such as those by Sallie Mae and Student Monitor, on student credit card use or indebtedness.[6] We assessed these data by interviewing Student Monitor and Sallie Mae officials knowledgeable about the data and checked the data for illogical values or obvious errors and found them to be sufficiently reliable for providing general information on student credit card use. Furthermore, we interviewed representatives of seven credit card issuers, which included the five largest general credit card issuers as determined by portfolio size in 2011. Four of these seven issuers offered affinity credit cards, representing 91 percent of the affinity card market in 2012, as measured by number of cardholders. Five of these seven issuers also offered student credit cards. Finally, we interviewed academics and representatives of federal agencies and other organizations that have studied issues related to college affinity cards or college students' credit card use. We conducted this performance audit from December 2012 to February 2014 in accordance with generally accepted government auditing standards. Those standards require that we plan and perform the audit to obtain sufficient, appropriate evidence to provide a reasonable basis for our findings and conclusions based on our audit objectives. We believe that the evidence obtained provides a reasonable basis for our findings and conclusions based on our audit objectives.

BACKGROUND

Almost 537 million general-purpose credit cards were in circulation in the United States as of the end of 2012.[7] Since at least the early 1990s, some credit card issuers have offered college affinity cards, which are governed by contracts (agreements) between the issuer and an organization such as a college, university, or alumni association. The cards typically bear the organization's logo. In return, the issuer makes payments to the organization based on factors such as the number of cards issued or the amount charged to the cards. College affinity cards can be an effective way for issuers to market credit cards because college alumni often have an attachment to their schools.

In addition, some credit card issuers, including banks and credit unions, offer college student credit cards—cards that are specifically labeled and intended for college students. As of November 2013, 6 of the 10 largest credit card issuers offered these cards, such as Citibank's Citi Dividend Card for College Students and Bank of America's BankAmericard Cash Rewards for Students.[8] Issuers use these cards to help build a base of customers who may continue using the issuers' credit cards after graduation. The terms and conditions of college student credit cards may be somewhat different from those of other credit cards—for example, they may have lower initial credit limits.[9]

In 2009, the CARD Act changed the marketing and terms and conditions of credit cards for young people, requiring additional consumer protections and disclosures for students and consumers under the age of 21.[10] Among other things, the act requires that

- any new credit card application for someone under 21 contain either (1) a co-signer over 21 who has the ability to make payments on the debts from the account and who will be jointly liable for debts incurred by the applicant until he or she is age 21, or (2) supporting information showing that the applicant would have the independent ability to make payments on any debt incurred from the use of the card (an "ability to pay");
- co-signers of such accounts approve increased credit lines until the cardholder is 21;
- card issuers not obtain a credit report for someone under 21 to use to make an unsolicited prescreened credit offer; and
- card issuers and creditors not offer a student any tangible item to induce the student to apply for or participate in a credit card on or near the campus of the institution of higher education or at an event sponsored by or related to an institution of higher education.

The act also requires credit card issuers to submit to CFPB each year the terms and conditions of any college affinity credit card agreement between the issuer and an institution of higher education or an affiliated organization in effect at any time during the preceding calendar year.[11] In addition to a copy of any college credit card agreement to which the issuer was a party, issuers also must submit summary information for each agreement, such as the number of cardholders covered with accounts open at year-end (regardless of when the account was opened) and the payments made by the issuer to the institution or organization during the year.[12] CFPB must submit to Congress, and make available to the public, an annual report that contains the information submitted by the card issuers to CFPB.[13] On December 17, 2013, CFPB issued the fourth annual report, which covered the 2012 calendar year.

CHANGES IN THE COLLEGE AFFINITY CARD MARKET SINCE THE CARD ACT

Number of Card Agreements, Cardholders, and Payments Declined in 2009–2012

Since the CARD Act was passed in 2009, the numbers of college affinity card agreements and cardholders have decreased, according to data from the Federal Reserve and CFPB. From 2009 through 2012, the number of card agreements declined from 1,045 to 617 (41 percent). Similarly, the total number of cardholders for college affinity cards declined by 40 percent (see table 1).

In 2012, 43 percent of the 617 college affinity card agreements were with alumni associations and 28 percent were with a college, university, or other institution of higher education (see figure 1).

Among these organization types, the greatest decline in the number of card agreements since 2009 was for institutions of higher education (see fig. 2).

In contrast, the largest decline in the number of overall cardholders occurred within alumni associations, while “other” organizations (a category that includes fraternities, sororities, and professional or trade organizations) had the largest decrease in the number of new cardholders (see table 2).

Table 1. College Affinity Card Agreements, Cardholders, and New Cardholders, 2009-2012

	2009	2010	2011	2012	Net change, 2009–2012	Percent change, 2009–2012
Number of agreements	1,045	1,005	796	617	(428)	-41%
Number of cardholders as of Dec. 31	2,041,511	1,709,054	1,503,664	1,222,718	(818,793)	-40%
Number of new cardholders	55,747	46,385	43,227	45,519	(10,228)	-18%

Source: CFPB.

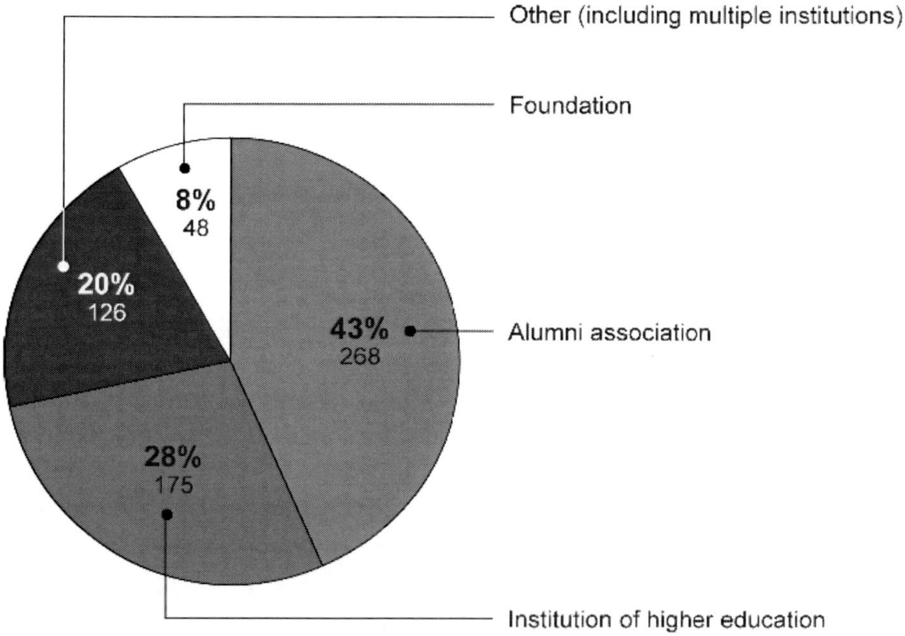

Source: GAO analysis of CFPB report.

Note: The percentages in the four categories do not add up to 100 percent due to rounding. "Other" includes fraternities, sororities, and professional or trade organizations, as well as agreements with multiple organizations, such as a university and an alumni association.

Figure 1. Prevalence of Affinity Card Agreements by Organization Type, 2012.

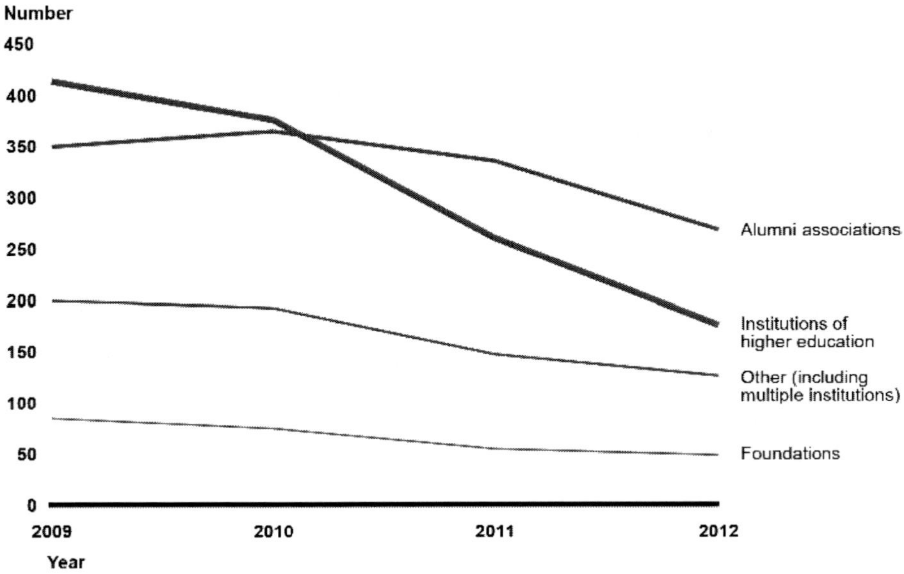

Source: GAO analysis of Federal Reserve and CFPB reports.

Figure 2. Number of Affinity Card Agreements, by Organization Type, 2009-2012.

Table 2. Affinity Card Agreements, Cardholders, and New Cardholders, by Organization Type, 2009-2012

	Number of agreements		**Number of cardholders**		**Number of new cardholders**	
	Net change	**% Change**	**Net change**	**% Change**	**Net change**	**% Change**
Alumni association	(81)	-23%	(290,196)	-28%	3,779	13%
Foundation	(36)	-43%	(55,238)	-41%	(2,137)	-53%
Institution of higher education	(238)	-58%	(230,732)	-51%	(4,077)	-32%
Other (including multiple organizations)	(73)	-37%	(242,627)	-57%	(7,793)	-73%
Total	**(428)**	**-41%**	**(818,793)**	**-40%**	**(10,228)**	**-18%**

Source: GAO analysis of Federal Reserve and CFPB reports.

Note: Reported numbers include corrections filed with the Federal Reserve and CFPB after the initial report was issued.

In 2012, 23 credit card issuers offered college affinity cards.[14] One issuer—FIA Card Services, N.A., a subsidiary of Bank of America—had 412 of the 617 reported agreements (67 percent of the market). However, as seen in figure 3, the company's market share has dropped since 2009.

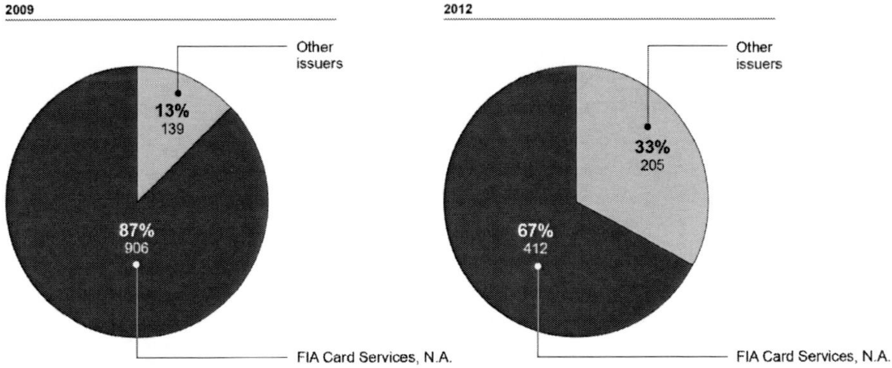

Source: GAO analysis of Federal Reserve and CFPB reports.

Figure 3. Number of Affinity Card Agreements, FIA Card Services and Other Issuers, 2009 and 2012.

Most affinity card issuers had a small number of card agreements—for example, the majority of issuers had one or two affinity card agreements (see table 3).

Table 3. Number of Agreements by Issuer, 2009-2012

	2009	2010	2011	2012	Net Change, 2009–2012
FIA Card Services, N.A.	906	848	633	412	(494)
Capital One Bank[a]	1	10	32	55	54
U.S. Bank National Association ND	60	54	51	48	(12)
UMB Bank, N.A.	6	23	22	39	33
Chase Bank USA, N.A.	36	28	17	15	(21)
Pennsylvania State Employees Credit Union	13	13	13	14	1
INTRUST Bank, N.A.	8	9	10	10	2
USAA Savings Bank	1	2	2	4	3
Compass Bank	1	2	3	2	1
GE Capital Retail Bank	3	2	2	2	(1)
Michigan State University Federal Credit Union	1	2	2	2	1

	2009	2010	2011	2012	Net Change, 2009–2012
Oregon Community Credit Union and OCCU Card Services, LLC	-	-	-	2	2
Pen Air Federal Credit Union	-	1	1	2	2
Banco Popular de Puerto Rico	1	1	1	1	-
Barclays Bank Delaware	1	1	1	1	-
Carolina Trust Federal Credit Union	-	1	1	1	1
Elevations Credit Union	1	1	1	1	-
MIT Credit Union	-	-	-	1	1
PNC Bank, National Association	2	2	1	1	(1)
Purdue Federal Credit Union	1	1	1	1	-
University of Illinois Employees Credit Union	-	1	1	1	1
USC Credit Union	-	1	1	1	1
Wright-Patt Credit Union, Inc.	-	-	-	1	1
Commerce Bank, N.A.	1	-	-	-	(1)
First National Bank of Omaha	2	2	-	-	(2)
Total	**1,045**	**1,005**	**796**	**617**	**(428)**

Source: GAO analysis of Federal Reserve and CFPB reports.
[a]Includes agreements filed by Capital One Bank (USA), N.A. and Capital One, N.A.

The payments that card issuers made to institutions with which they had affinity card agreements have decreased since 2009, consistent with the decline in the number of agreements and cardholders.[15] As shown in table 4, affinity card issuers made payments of $50.4 million to participating institutions in 2012. The median payment in 2012 was about $5,000, while the average (mean) was about $82,000, with alumni associations receiving the highest average payment.

Table 4. Total Payments, Average Payments, and Median Payments from Affinity Card Issuers to Organizations, by Organization Type, 2012

	Total payments	Average payment	Median payment	Range
Alumni association	$30,805,378	$115,376	$6,163	$0 - $2,742,743
Institution of higher education	11,791,359	67,379	3,252	0 - 1,505,550
Other	4,239,222	33,645	6,413	0 - 898,924
Foundation	3,560,142	74,170	1,833	0 -1,157,737
Total (overall)	**$50,396,102**	**$ 81,812**	**$ 5,062**	**$0 - $2,742,743**

Source: GAO analysis of CFPB data.

Note: Numbers may not add to the shown total because of rounding.

Total payments declined by 40 percent between 2009 and 2012. The largest decline in payments was to alumni associations, while institutions of higher education had the largest decline in affinity card agreements over this period. However, during that period, the average payment to institutions of higher education increased by about $13,200, while the average payment to alumni associations decreased by about $13,700. The University of Southern California, through its agreement with FIA Card Services, received about $1.5 million, the largest payment to an institution of higher education in 2012. Among all the organizations, the Penn State Alumni Association received the largest payment in 2012— about $2.7 million, from FIA Card Services. In contrast, 22 percent of the agreements did not result in any payments to organizations in 2012.

Card Agreements Can Cover Target Customers, Payments, and Marketing Practices

College affinity card agreements serve as contracts between the card issuer and the participating organization. Using a data collection instrument, we reviewed 39 agreements filed with CFPB, which represented about 38 percent of all cardholders covered by college affinity card agreements in 2011.[16] The agreements typically covered such things as the card's target market, marketing practices, and payments to the participating organization. As shown in figure 4, the length of time that the card agreements had been in effect varied. The oldest originally was signed in January 1991 and the most recent in December 2011. Many of the agreements had been amended or received addendums since they were first adopted, which in some cases extended the existing terms of the original agreement. In addition to credit cards, 30 of the 39 agreements included other financial products, such as deposit and checking accounts, automobile and home loans, and investment accounts. Some agreements included exclusivity provisions that restricted the organization from offering its members these products except in conjunction with the current affinity card issuer.

Target Customers and Marketing Practices

The agreements identified which potential cardholders the issuer could solicit and how. Thirty-seven of the 39 reviewed agreements identified specific target customers for the college affinity card. Most often, issuers targeted alumni for the cards, but two-thirds of the agreements also allowed the issuers to solicit undergraduate students (see table 5).[17] Most of the agreements identified multiple target populations for card solicitations.

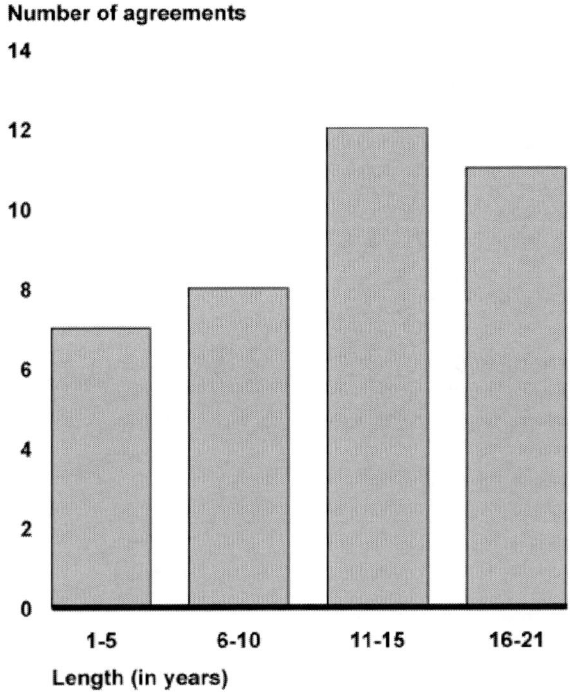

Source: GAO.

Note: One of the 39 agreements we reviewed did not include dates and is not included in this analysis.

Figure 4. Length of Time (in Years) That Organizations Had a College Affinity Card Agreement, for 38 Agreements Reviewed.

All but two of the 39 reviewed agreements included provisions requiring the organization to provide a list of its members to the issuer for marketing purposes. However, two-thirds of the agreements included mechanisms allowing the organizations to exclude members who requested that they not receive third-party solicitations. Nine of the reviewed agreements also included restrictions on soliciting student members, generally by restricting their inclusion on the provided lists.

The agreements allowed card issuers to solicit potential cardholders through a variety of methods (see table 6). More than 80 percent of the reviewed agreements allowed issuers to use telemarketing, website links (such as from the alumni association's website), direct mail, and print advertisements (such as in sport programs or member magazines). All of the reviewed agreements allowed the issuers to use more than one of the different methods that we tracked.

Table 5. Prevalence of Target Markets/Members in 39 Reviewed Agreements

Target market	Number of agreements identifying this target market
Alumni	35
Students (undergraduate)	26
Employees	22
Season ticket holders/fans	22
Donors or friends	22
Parents	10
Other (graduate students, organization members, etc.)	23

Source: GAO.

Note: Agreements often cited more than one target market.

Table 6. Prevalence of Marketing Approaches in 39 Reviewed Agreements

Marketing method	Number of agreements including this marketing method
Use of trademark/logo/mascot	39
Print advertisements	37
Direct mail	37
Links on website	34
Telemarketing	32
Access to campus	30
E-mail or Internet solicitations	30

Source: GAO.

Note: Agreements included more than one marketing method.

All of the reviewed agreements included provisions allowing the card issuers to use the trademark or logo of the institution of higher education or organization. In some instances, the issuer could put these trademarks on gifts for individuals who completed applications or on other items. All but two of the agreements included provisions for obtaining prior approval of marketing materials from the organization or institution (to help ensure that the card issuer used the trademark or logo appropriately).

Payments to Organizations under the Agreements

All but one of the 39 reviewed agreements contained information about the payment arrangement between the issuer and the affiliated organization or institution of higher education. As shown in table 7, issuers most frequently provided payments to the organization or institution based on the number of new and open cards and the amount of money charged to the cards. Many included bonus payments for accounts that the organization or institution originated (as opposed to ones originated through the issuer), and three included bonus payments if the number of cardholders exceeded a threshold. Many of the agreements also included a guaranteed payment to the organization or institution that was not based on the number of cardholders or amount charged.

Table 7. Prevalence of Payment Types in 39 Reviewed Agreements

Type of payment	Number of agreements including this payment type
Payment per new card	31
Payment based on number of open cards	31
Payment based on spending volume	31
Guaranteed payment	27
Payment for funded savings or checking account	16

Source: GAO.

Note: Agreements often included more than one type of payment.

The reviewed agreements sometimes contained payments based on other related products or included broader financial support to the organization or institution. For example, some payments under the agreements were based on balances of certificates of deposit or loans provided. In some instances, the reviewed agreements included support for scholarships or building renovations.

Consumer Protections and Service Standards

About one-quarter of the 39 reviewed agreements included explicit consumer or cardholder protections or service standards. The consumer protections included restrictions on how often and how issuers could solicit group members, as well as restrictions on the sharing of the member database or student information with third parties. Two of the reviewed agreements also included metrics to assess servicing standards. For example, one agreement with an alumni association specified how quickly the issuer would answer and resolve calls and also required that the credit card terms and features (such as fees and annual percentage rates) be "best in class" when compared with a set of identified peer institutions. Additionally, most of the reviewed agreements included provisions allowing the issuer to make periodic adjustments to the card program and its terms and features.

Marketing to Students Appears to Have Declined

According to available data and representatives of card issuers and affiliated organizations, marketing of college affinity cards and college student credit cards directly to students appears to have declined.

Largest Issuers of Affinity Credit Cards Stated They No Longer Marketed the Cards Directly to Students

As of 2013, college affinity cards were not being marketed directly to students, according to representatives of issuers and affiliated organizations with whom we spoke. Four large issuers of affinity cards, representing 91 percent of the market (as measured by 2012 cardholders), said they did not actively market these cards to students— that is, they did not market on campus or specifically target students through direct mail, e-mail, print or broadcast media, or their other marketing venues.[18] Representatives of five affiliated organizations with affinity credit card agreements corroborated these statements; they told us that the card issuers no longer marketed their affinity cards to students, focusing instead on alumni. The issuers noted that it was still possible that some students applied for college affinity cards because they would see the same marketing as the general public—such as advertising at bank branches, sporting events, or on issuer websites. Graduate students also may receive card solicitations from their undergraduate schools or alumni organizations. Officials from three affiliated organizations estimated that the percentage of their current cardholders who still were students was less than 3 percent and that these percentages had been declining.

Before the enactment of the CARD Act in 2009, it was not uncommon for college affinity cards to be marketed to students. Representatives of four organizations with college affinity cards told us that at one time their cards were targeted to students, and, as discussed earlier, card agreements often specified students as a target market and required sharing student contact information for marketing purposes. However, many of the new agreements—and amendments to existing agreements—we reviewed that were put in place after 2009 expressly limit or restrict the marketing of college affinity cards to students.

Views diverged on the extent to which the CARD Act was responsible for the decline in marketing of college affinity cards to students. One card issuer told us the act had little influence because the company had begun reducing marketing cards to students before the statute was enacted. A second issuer said it did not market to students because it sought more affluent customers, but it acknowledged the CARD Act also played a role by making it more difficult and less efficient to market to students—for example, placing restrictions on making prescreened credit offers to those under 21. Representatives of three organizations with college affinity cards told us they believed the CARD Act played a significant role in the decline of card marketing to students. Institutions of higher education also may have influenced this decline—for example, representatives of one college told us that undergraduate students were not included in its program or targeted for marketing, largely because the college did not want to be seen as pushing credit cards on its students.

Marketing of college affinity cards overall—not just to students—has declined in recent years as many large issuers have diminished their presence in the marketplace. As discussed earlier, the number of agreements and cardholders declined by 41 percent and 40 percent, respectively, from 2009 through 2012. Three of the four affinity card issuers told us they were not actively seeking additional agreements. Specifically, one issuer said it was exiting the marketplace as existing agreements expired, one said it was evaluating the performance of its existing portfolio before deciding a future direction, and one said it was evaluating each agreement as it expired and did not regard its college affinity card business as strategically important. The fourth issuer noted that while it was seeking new agreements, it had ended many of its existing agreements because it did not see the program being sustainable over the long term.

Although some card agreements provide payments to the affiliated organizations based on the number of card accounts, organizations told us they generally played a limited role in marketing the cards to their members. Three of the five organizations had sent e-mails to their members promoting the cards. One of these organizations told us it would like to do additional marketing of its own but that the issuer had been reluctant to permit this. Two organizations were concerned that participation in marketing could affect the tax status of their payments under the agreements.[19]

Marketing of Credit Cards Specifically to Students Has Declined, According to Issuers and Survey Data

Active marketing of college student credit cards appears to have declined in recent years. We spoke with five issuers of these cards, which represented 39 percent of all general-purpose credit cards in circulation as of December 2012.[20] All the issuers told us that as of 2013, they did not rely on active marketing to students to solicit potential cardholders. Active marketing includes methods such as direct mail, telemarketing, or e-mail. Instead, interested students could learn about the cards through issuer or third-party websites and bank branch offices.

Representatives of affiliated organizations with whom we spoke confirmed they had observed a reduction in the marketing of credit cards to students in recent years. For example, they noted that issuers no longer conducted on-campus solicitations at sporting events and other university functions, as they had in the past. Two organizations told us they believed the decline in marketing of college student credit cards began by the early or mid-2000s, while three others said it began around 2009, when the CARD Act was enacted.

According to annual surveys of college students conducted by Student Monitor, a market research firm specializing in the college student market, the number of students obtaining a credit card in response to a solicitation through direct mail or on campus has dropped significantly in recent years.[21] The proportion of students reporting that they obtained a credit card as a result of a direct mail solicitation declined from 36 percent in 2000 to 6 percent in 2013 (see fig. 5).[22] In 2013, students reported receiving significantly fewer mail (1.6) and e-mail solicitations (1.4) in a typical month than respondents in 2007

(5.6 and 9.1, respectively). Two issuers told us the decline in direct mail resulted in part from restrictions in the CARD Act on prescreened credit offers to those under 21. In 2013, fewer than 1 percent of students obtained their credit card as a result of an on-campus display or a company representative on campus (a practice known as tabling), as compared with 15 percent and 6 percent, respectively, in 2000. Two issuers told us they still used on-campus marketing but that they focused on their other financial products, such as checking accounts, and no longer accepted credit card applications at on-campus events.

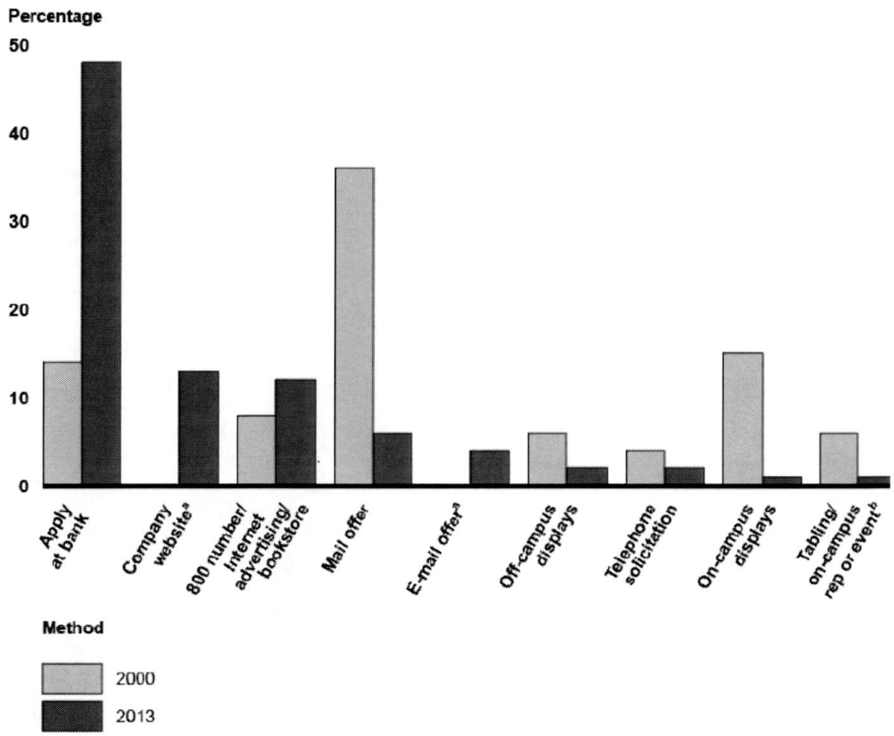

Source: Student Monitor.

[a] Data not available for 2000.

[b]Tabling refers to staffing tables at a campus location to market credit cards to students.

Figure 5. Percentage of Students Obtaining Their Credit Cards, by Method of Solicitation, 2000 and 2013.

According to Student Monitor, more students have been acquiring their credit cards by initiating contact with the card issuer. For example, in 2013, 48 percent of students receiving a credit card applied in person at a bank (often the one with which they already had a deposit account), compared with 14 percent in 2000. Twenty-four percent received a card by initiating contact through the Internet or by telephone, compared with approximately 8 percent in 2000.

EFFECT OF COLLEGE AFFINITY AND STUDENT CARDS ON STUDENT CREDIT CARD DEBT LARGELY IS UNKNOWN

Data are not available to definitively determine the effect that affinity cards and college student cards have had on student credit card debt. The effect of affinity cards may be limited because, as seen earlier, fewer students appear to hold these cards. The effect of college student cards is difficult to determine because the available data cover credit cards in general rather than college student cards in particular. However, students' overall use of credit cards appears to have declined in recent years.

Limited Information Available on Effects of College Affinity and Student Credit Cards on Card Debt

Publicly available data do not allow a clear determination of the impact of college affinity and college student cards on student credit card debt. One limiting factor is that card issuers do not always ask on applications or know which of their cardholders are students. Additionally, while some data exist about the age of credit cardholders, age is not a reliable proxy for student status, especially as the age of college students has increased in recent years.[23] Multiple studies have examined the factors influencing credit card use among students, but none that we identified focused specifically on the impact of college affinity or college student credit cards on student debt. For example, a 2012 study that examined the effect of the CARD Act reviewed affinity card agreements and surveyed college students on their use of credit cards, but it did not seek to determine the impact of particular types of credit cards.[24] Similarly, surveys on student credit card use by Sallie Mae (a financial services company specializing in education) and Student Monitor, discussed later in this report, asked respondents about general credit card use but not specifically about affinity or college student credit cards.

College Affinity Cards

The effect of affinity cards on student credit card debt may be limited because fewer students appear to hold these cards, which generally have not been marketed specifically to college students since at least 2009. Representatives of two organizations with affinity cards estimated that 1 percent or less of their current cardholders were students, while a third organization estimated that 3 percent were students. The proportion of affinity cards held by students appears to have declined since the cards' introduction. For example, one organization estimated that in the past, up to 15 percent of its cardholders were students, but that virtually none were at present.

However, the exact prevalence of students holding affinity credit cards is not known. While the CARD Act requires issuers to submit information on college affinity card programs, including the number of cardholders, to CFPB, issuers are not required to report on the number of student cardholders. Three affinity card issuers with whom we spoke said that they could not identify which cardholders were students, or they considered cardholder information proprietary and therefore declined to share the information.

College Student Credit Cards

We did not identify data that would allow a determination of the effect of college student credit cards in particular—as distinct from credit cards in general—on student credit card debt. Representatives of CFPB, researchers, and organizations that have studied credit card use told us that they were not aware of research or data sets specific to college student credit cards. While banks file quarterly reports with regulators that contain information on the banks' credit card portfolios, these reports do not differentiate by type of card.[25] Similarly, *The Nilson Report*, an industry trade journal that reports on credit cards, has not issued a report specific to student credit cards in more than 10 years. Four issuers of college student credit cards told us they were unable to share specific information on these cards or the student holders of their other credit cards because the information was not available or they considered such information proprietary.[26] Even if comprehensive data on college student credit cards existed, the data's value for understanding student credit card debt would be limited because many cardholders could continue to use their student cards after they ceased being students.

Students' Overall Use of Credit Cards Appears to Have Declined

While data specific to college affinity and college student credit cards are limited, available evidence suggests college students' use of credit cards overall has declined in recent years. Annual surveys of college students conducted by Sallie Mae and Student Monitor represent two primary sources of information on student credit card use.[27]

Number of Students with Credit Cards

The two studies suggest that the number of students owning credit cards declined in recent years. Student Monitor found that the proportion of college students holding credit cards declined from 53 percent in 2004 to 33 percent in 2013.[28] Sallie Mae reported the proportion of students owning credit cards decreased from 49 percent in 2010 (the first year it began collecting this information) to 29 percent in 2013 (see fig. 6).[29] In the Student Monitor study, 72 percent of students who had a credit card in their own name in 2013 owned a single card, 21 percent had two credit cards, and 8 percent had three or more credit cards.

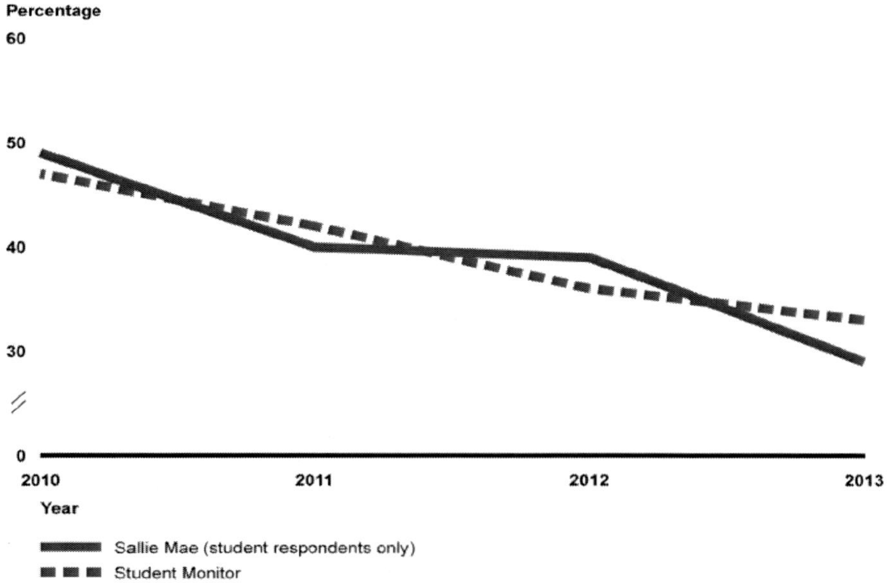

Source: GAO analysis of Sallie Mae and Student Monitor reports.

Figure 6. Percent of Students Who Reported Owning a Credit Card, 2010-2013.

CFPB and the Federal Reserve Bank of Richmond similarly reported a decline in credit card ownership among younger consumers. In a 2013 CFPB survey of major credit card issuers, new cards issued to those under 21 dropped from 3.9 million in 2007 to 1.7 million in 2012 (a 56 percent reduction). The percentage of consumers ages 18-20 who opened a credit card account dropped from 33.6 percent to 14.4 percent during that period.[30] The study by the Federal Reserve Bank of Richmond analyzed consumer credit data and found that individuals under 21 were 8 percentage points less likely to have a credit card after the CARD Act than before it became law in 2009.[31]

At the same time, students who get credit cards in their own names—that is, the students receive the bill and are responsible for payment— increasingly have been doing so before starting college. According to Student Monitor, 56 percent of students in 2013 obtained their first credit card before starting college—29 percent in high school or earlier, and 27 percent between high school and college (see fig. 7).[32] In contrast, in 2000, students were more likely to get their first credit card when they already were in college.

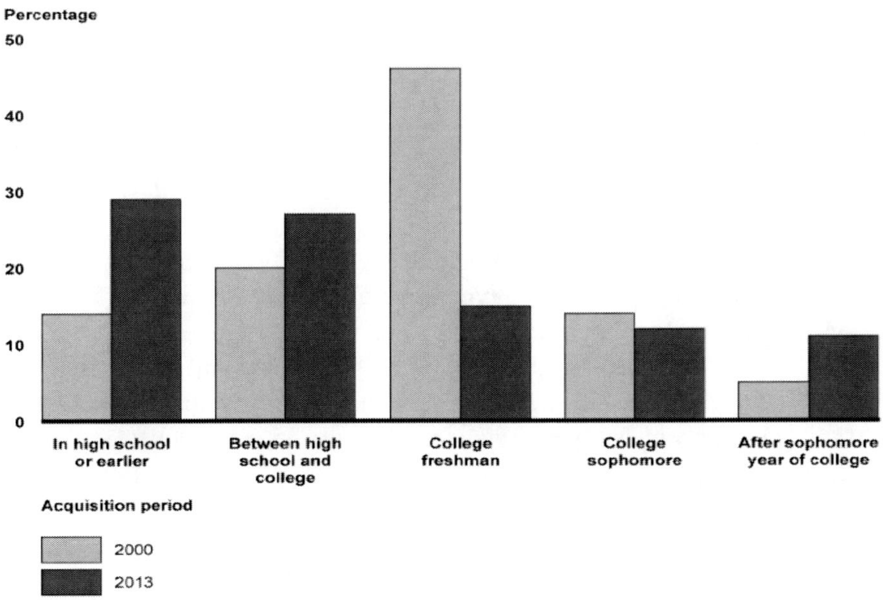

Source: Student Monitor.

Note: The data above include only those credit cards for which the student is responsible for payment.

Figure 7. Time Period of Credit Card Acquisition for Students with Credit Cards, 2000 and 2013.

While students' use of credit cards appears to have declined, their use of debit cards has increased. According to Student Monitor, 63 percent of students had a debit card in 2013, as compared with 59 percent in 2008 and 51 percent in 2000. Representatives of the financial industry and a researcher told us that the recent financial crisis has made many students and younger people more wary of credit and thus more disposed to using prepaid and debit cards. Student Monitor found that 62 percent of students interviewed in 2013 said they feared getting into credit card debt.

Charges and Balances

Forty-five percent of all students with a credit card in their name charged $100 or less each month in 2013, according to Student Monitor. Fifty-nine percent used their card fewer than six times a month, including 8 percent who indicated that they did not usually use their credit card each month. On average, students charged $171 monthly, a decrease of 8 percent from 2012.

Sallie Mae reported that students' median reported balance for all cardholders was $179 in 2013, as compared with $289 in 2011. The survey also found that 2 percent of all students in 2013 with a credit card had a combined outstanding balance of more than $4,000, while 29 percent had a zero balance. Student Monitor found that the 28 percent of respondents who carried a balance had a median outstanding balance of $136.

Credit Limits

Credit limits for credit cards owned by students usually are lower than those for the general population and have been decreasing. In 2010, the median credit limit for all bank-type general credit cards was $15,000.[33] In contrast, Student Monitor found that more than 60 percent of credit cards owned by students had credit limits of $500 or less, and 80 percent were $1,000 or less. In 2000, 27 percent of respondents had credit limits of $1,000 or less, and 11 percent had limits of at least $5,000. However, because students may have multiple credit cards, their total credit card debt can be higher than the credit limit of any one card.

Payment and Delinquency Patterns

Several studies provide information on college students' payment patterns for credit cards:

- *Payment amount.* Student Monitor found that 72 percent of students reported paying their outstanding charges in full each month in 2013.

Sallie Mae found that 52 percent of student respondents in 2013 paid in full each month in the previous year, and that 10 percent of students typically made only the minimum payment.[34]

- *Parental responsibility*. The Student Monitor and Sallie Mae studies found that the college student, rather than the parent, was most often responsible for making credit card payments (79 percent in the Student Monitor study and 92 percent in the Sallie Mae study).
- *Late payment fees*. One quarter of students in the 2013 Student Monitor study reported paying a late payment fee at least once since acquiring a credit card, with almost half of that group incurring more than one late fee.
- *Delinquent payment*. Cardholders under 21 were more likely to experience minor delinquencies (30 or 60 days past due) than older cardholders, according to the Federal Reserve Bank of Richmond study.[35] At the same time, young cardholders were substantially less likely to experience serious delinquency (90 days past due and longer). The study also found that cardholders who got their credit cards earlier in life were less likely to experience a serious default later in life.

AGENCY COMMENTS

We provided a draft of this report to CFPB and the Federal Reserve. We incorporated technical comments from these agencies as appropriate.

Alicia Puente Cackley
Director, Financial Markets and Community Investment

APPENDIX I: OBJECTIVES, SCOPE, AND METHODOLOGY

This report examines (1) the trends associated with and characteristics of college affinity card agreements, (2) the extent of marketing for college affinity and college student credit cards, and (3) what is known about the effect of the use of affinity cards and student credit cards on student credit card debt. We use "college affinity card" to refer to a credit card issued in conjunction with an agreement between a credit card issuer and an institution of higher education or an affiliated organization (such as an alumni association or foundation). We use "college student credit card" to refer to a credit card established for and targeted to college students.

To identify the trends and general characteristics associated with college affinity card agreements, we reviewed the 2010 and 2011 *Report to the Congress on College Credit Card Agreements*, which the Board of Governors of the Federal Reserve System (Federal Reserve) issued, and the 2012 and 2013 *College Credit Card Agreements: Annual Report to Congress*, which the Bureau of Consumer Financial Protection (also known as the Consumer Financial Protection Bureau or CFPB) issued.[1] These reports provide summary information, such as the total number of agreements in effect and number of accounts open at the end of the year.[2]

To determine the characteristics of the agreements, we first reviewed and analyzed affinity card agreements between issuers and schools or affiliated organizations from calendar years 2009-2012. We downloaded information for all those agreements in effect during those years from public databases managed by the Federal Reserve and CFPB.[3] We analyzed the agreements to identify general trends and characteristics. We assessed these data by interviewing Federal Reserve and CFPB staff knowledgeable about the data and checking the data for illogical values or obvious errors. We found the data to be sufficiently reliable for describing the general characteristics and trends of the affinity card marketplace. Because we were most interested in current agreements, we focused our analysis on the agreements from 2011, the most recent year for which information was available. Twenty providers issued these agreements.[4] For a more thorough analysis, we selected a nonprobability sample of 39 agreements from 574 agreements identified as being in effect as of January 1, 2012.[5] We determined the sample by applying three criteria to the agreements. First, we included the 25 largest agreements overall, as measured by the number of cardholders. Second, we included the largest agreement from each issuer that provided affinity credit cards.[6] Third, we included the five largest agreements with institutions of higher education, as measured by the number of cardholders under those agreements. These numbers do not add to 39 because agreements could meet criteria for inclusion under more than one category. We selected these criteria because we wanted to capture a large proportion of affinity cardholders as well as any potential variation among issuers or organizational type. We included the five largest institutions of higher education because we anticipated that those agreements could be more likely to include students as cardholders, a topic of specific interest. See table 8 for the list of reviewed agreements.

Table 8. 2011 College Credit Card Agreements Selected for Review, by Institution Type, Issuer, and Size Categories

Institution or organization	Type of institution or organization	Credit card issuer	Largest 25 agreements, by number of cardholders	Largest agreement for issuer, by number of cardholders	Largest five agreements with universities, by number of cardholders
Penn State Alumni Association	Alumni association	FIA Card Services, N.A.[a]	Yes	Yes	No
Golden Key International Honour Society	Other	FIA Card Services, N.A.	Yes	No	No
Alumni Association of the University of Michigan	Alumni association	FIA Card Services, N.A.	Yes	No	No
Association of Former Students of Texas AM University	Alumni association	FIA Card Services, N.A.	Yes	No	No
The Ex-Students Association of the University of Texas	Alumni association	FIA Card Services, N.A.	Yes	No	No
Indiana University Alumni Association	Alumni association	FIA Card Services, N.A.	Yes	No	No
UCLA Alumni Association	Alumni association	FIA Card Services, N.A.	Yes	No	No
Wisconsin Alumni Association	Alumni association	FIA Card Services, N.A.	Yes	No	No
University of Southern California	University	FIA Card Services, N.A.	Yes	No	Yes
The University of Georgia Foundation	Foundation	FIA Card Services, N.A.	Yes	No	No

Table 8. (Continued)

Institution or organization	Type of institution or organization	Credit card issuer	Largest 25 agreements, by number of cardholders	Largest agreement for issuer, by number of cardholders	Largest five agreements with universities, by number of cardholders
California Alumni Association	Alumni association	FIA Card Services, N.A.	Yes	No	No
General Alumni Association of University of North Carolina at Chapel Hill	Alumni association	FIA Card Services, N.A.	Yes	No	No
Purdue Alumni Association	Alumni association	Purdue Federal Credit Union	Yes	Yes	No
University of Puerto Rico	University	Banco Popular de Puerto Rico	Yes	Yes	Yes
State University of Iowa Alumni Association	Alumni association	FIA Card Services, N.A.	Yes	No	No
The Ohio State University Alumni Association, Inc.	Alumni association	FIA Card Services, N.A.	Yes	No	No
Stanford Alumni Association	Alumni association	FIA Card Services, N.A.	Yes	No	No
Phi Theta Kappa International Honor Society	Other	FIA Card Services, N.A.	Yes	No	No
Auburn Spirit Foundation	Foundation	FIA Card Services, N.A.	Yes	No	No
Iowa State University Alumni Association	Alumni association	FIA Card Services, N.A.	Yes	No	No

Institution or organization	Type of institution or organization	Credit card issuer	Largest 25 agreements, by number of cardholders	Largest agreement for issuer, by number of cardholders	Largest five agreements with universities, by number of cardholders
National Alumni Association of the University of Alabama	Alumni association	FIA Card Services, N.A.	Yes	No	No
Clemson University, Inc.	Alumni association	FIA Card Services, N.A.	Yes	No	No
University of Arizona Alumni Association	Alumni association	FIA Card Services, N.A.	Yes	No	No
Kansas State University Alumni Association	Alumni	INTRUST Bank, N.A.	Yes	Yes	No
Trustees of the University of Pennsylvania	University	FIA Card Services, N.A.	Yes	No	Yes
Virginia Tech Alumni Association	Alumni association	Chase Bank USA, N.A.	No	Yes	No
Harvard Alumni Association	Alumni association	Barclays Bank Delaware	No	Yes	No
Boston University	Alumni association	U.S. Bank National Association ND	No	Yes	No
University of Illinois Alumni Association	Alumni association	University of Illinois Employees Credit Union	No	Yes	No
Western Michigan Alumni Association	Alumni association	PNC Bank, National Association	No	Yes	No

Table 8. (Continued)

Institution or organization	Type of institution or organization	Credit card issuer	Largest 25 agreements, by number of cardholders	Largest agreement for issuer, by number of cardholders	Largest five agreements with universities, by number of cardholders
Michigan State University	University	Michigan State University Federal Credit Union	No	Yes	No
Georgia Tech Alumni Association	Alumni association	Capital One, N.A.	No	Yes	No
Association of Graduates of the United States Air Force Academy	Alumni association	USAA Savings Bank	No	Yes	No
Boston College	University	GE Money Bank	No	Yes	No
The Principia	Alumni association	UMB Bank, N.A.	No	Yes	No
Coastal Carolina University	University	Carolina Trust FCU	No	Yes	No
University of West Florida Foundation Inc	Foundation	Pen Air Federal Credit Union	No	Yes	No
The Trustees of Columbia University	University	FIA Card Services, N.A.	No	No	Yes
St Johns University New York	University	FIA Card Services, N.A.	No	No	Yes
Total			25	16	5

Source: GAO analysis of CFPB data.
[a]FIA Card Services, N.A. is a subsidiary of Bank of America.

Collectively, the agreements included in our sample covered about 38 percent of all cardholders in 2011. Twenty-six of the reviewed agreements were with alumni associations, 8 were with institutions of higher education, 3 were with foundations, and 2 were with other organizations.

We reviewed these agreements and collected information using a data collection instrument (DCI) to gather characteristics such as their effective date, duration, allowed marketing practices and target populations, payments to the organization, consumer protections, and service standards. Findings from this limited review of 39 agreements cannot be generalized to the overall population of agreements in 2011.

We developed the DCI after reviewing some of the 2011 agreements, focusing on items such as the scope, consumer protections, marketing practices, payments, terms, and fees. We converted the DCI to a pdf format for direct data entry. Three team members entered information on two agreements each using the DCI and discussed their experiences. We revised some questions for clarity and deleted others to avoid duplication. This version of the DCI was reviewed by a GAO survey specialist and an expert who surveyed students regarding their credit card use and conducted a similar review of the credit card agreements, and we incorporated minor changes. We further clarified that the review of agreements would focus on the most recent full agreement or amendment and those items that were still in effect as of January 1, 2012. Two team members then entered information about the agreements into the DCI. We verified our coding by comparing the original coder's DCI responses with those of the second coder. For each comparison set, we compared the coding for 59 data elements and found discrepancies in fewer than 10 percent of the entries. This was determined to ensure a base level of reliability in the information collected. While the results of our review of the 39 agreements cannot be projected nationwide, they provide context and information related to the contents of the 39 agreements.

To address the second and third objectives, we reviewed documents and interviewed representatives of credit card issuers, organizations and schools with affinity card agreements, and federal agencies, as well as academics and other individuals who have studied credit cards and their use by students. We reviewed studies—such as those by Sallie Mae (a financial services company specializing in education), Student Monitor (a market research firm that specializes in the college student market), and U.S. Public Interest Research Group (a consumer advocacy organization)—on student credit card use. We identified these studies through the Econ Lit database and general Internet searches using terms such as "college credit cards." We focused on several years of Sallie Mae's *How America Pays for College* studies and on Student Monitor's *Financial Services – Spring 2013* report, as well as recent reports by CFPB and the Federal Reserve Bank of Richmond.[7] We assessed the quality of the survey data by interviewing Student Monitor and Sallie Mae officials knowledgeable about the data and checked the data for illogical values or obvious errors. We found the data to be of sufficient quality and reliability for providing general information on student credit card use. According to the Student Monitor, the estimates from the 2013 study had a 2.4 percent margin of error at the 95 percent confidence level. Because surveys are based on self-reporting of payment behaviors and estimated credit card debt levels, they may be prone to biases and not accurately represent actual behaviors and debt levels. The surveys were not designed to verify that information. Some researchers maintain that respondents sometimes underreport the quantity or level of characteristics that could be considered unflattering, such as the amount of outstanding credit card debt. We also reviewed marketing materials issuers used to market the cards. Lastly, we reviewed provisions of the Credit Card Accountability Responsibility and Disclosure Act of 2009 related to affinity credit cards and credit card use by those under 21.[8]

We interviewed representatives of four issuers of affinity credit cards—Bank of America (FIA Services), Capital One, Chase, and U.S. Bank— that had 91 percent of such cardholders in 2012. We also interviewed representatives of the five largest general credit card issuers, measured by 2011 portfolio size, as reported by *The Nilson Report*.[9] We discussed with these issuers—American Express, Bank of America (FIA Services), Chase, Citibank, and Wells Fargo—any student credit cards currently or previously issued. To get a broader perspective on the use of these cards by financial institutions, we also interviewed representatives of three industry trade groups—the American Bankers Association, the Consumer Bankers Association, and the Credit Union National Association.

We also interviewed representatives of six organizations and schools to discuss their affinity credit card relationships—the Association of Former Students of Texas A&M University, Boston University Alumni Association, Georgia Tech Alumni Association, Golden Key International Honour Society, Penn State Alumni Association, and Washington University. These six organizations were chosen because they had among the largest number of affinity cards (as determined by number of cardholders), had cards from the three affinity card issuers with the most agreements, and included one organization (Washington University) that had previously chosen to end its affinity agreement. To get a broader perspective, we also interviewed representatives of the National Association of College and University Business Officers.

In addition, we interviewed representatives of CFPB, the Department of Education, the Federal Reserve, and the Office of the Comptroller of the Currency to discuss their oversight of affinity and student credit cards and trends they have observed in the industry. We talked with two academics who have studied and written about student credit card use, as well as representatives of Sallie Mae, Student Monitor, and the U.S. Public Interest Research Group.

We conducted this performance audit from December 2012 to February 2014 in accordance with generally accepted government auditing standards. Those standards require that we plan and perform the audit to obtain sufficient, appropriate evidence to provide a reasonable basis for our findings and conclusions based on our audit objectives. We believe that the evidence obtained provides a reasonable basis for our findings and conclusions based on our audit objectives.

End Notes

[1] We conducted a separate review on debit and prepaid cards offered to students through agreements between schools and financial service providers. GAO, *College Debit Cards: Actions Needed to Address ATM Access, Student Choice, and Transparency*, GAO-14-91 (Washington, D.C.: Feb. 13, 2014).

[2] Pub. L. No. 111-24, 123 Stat. 1734.

[3] § 305(a), 123 Stat. at 1749-50 (codified at 15 U.S.C. § 1637(r)(2)).

[4] The CARD Act mandates that we review the annual reports submitted by card issuers as well as their marketing practices to determine the impact that college affinity card agreements and college student card agreements have on credit card debt. § 305(b), 123 Stat. at 1750-51.

[5] Results from nonprobability samples cannot be used to make inferences about a population, because in a nonprobability sample some elements of a population being studied have no chance or an unknown chance of being selected as part of the sample.

[6] Sallie Mae originates and services loans to and collects loans from students and families to help them finance the cost of their education. Student Monitor is a market research firm focused exclusively on the student marketplace.

[7] *The Nilson Report*, no. 1012 (February 2013).

[8] Largest credit card issuers as measured by the number of general-purpose credit cards in circulation in 2012, the most recent year for which data were available, according to *The Nilson Report*, no. 1012 (February 2013). The six issuers were Capital One Financial Corporation, Citigroup Inc., Bank of America Corporation, Discover Financial Services, U.S. Bancorp, Wells Fargo & Company, and Barclays Bank Delaware.

[9] We previously reported on college students' credit card use in 2001. See GAO, *Consumer Finance: College Students and Credit Cards*, GAO-01-773 (Washington, D.C.: June 20, 2001).

[10] Pub. L. No. 111-24, §§ 301-304, 123 Stat. 1734,1747-49.

[11] § 305(a); 12 C.F.R. § 1026.57(d). Implementation of the CARD Act, including receipt of the issuer submissions, was vested originally with the Federal Reserve but transferred to CFPB on July 21, 2011, pursuant to the Dodd-Frank Wall Street Reform and Consumer Protection Act, Pub. L. No. 111-203, 124 Stat. 1376 (2010).

[12] § 305(a): 12 C.F.R. § 1026.57(d). Issuers also must provide the number of new cardholders who opened accounts during the year, and any memorandum of understanding between the issuer and school or affiliated organization that directly or indirectly relates to any aspect of the agreement. *Id.*

[13] § 305(a). The Federal Reserve submitted the 2009 and 2010 reports, and CFPB submitted the 2011 and 2012 reports.

[14] We counted two entities that filed agreements separately–Capital One Bank (USA), N.A. and Capital One, N.A.–as a single issuer because both are subsidiaries of Capital One Financial Corporation.

[15] Because some agreements include the provision of financial products (such as deposit accounts) in addition to credit cards, payments made by issuers under these agreements may not relate solely to credit card accounts.

[16] Many of the agreements we reviewed contained multiple amendments or addendums. We focused our review on the most recent full agreement or amendment and those items that were still in effect. See appendix I for a list of the agreements we reviewed.

[17] As discussed later, while many agreements allow students to be a target market for the affinity cards, all of the issuers and affiliated organizations with which we spoke told us that, in practice, no issuers actively market to students at the present time.

[18] One of the four issuers noted that because it was planning to exit the college affinity card marketplace, it was no longer marketing its affinity credit cards to any population.

[19] An organization that is recognized as tax exempt may still be liable for tax on its unrelated business income, which is income from an activity that is not substantially related to the educational, charitable, or other purpose that is the basis of the organization's exemption.

[20] *The Nilson Report*. Because we did not identify an aggregate data source specifically for college student credit cards, it is not known what proportion of that market these issuers represent. In addition, representatives of one of the five issuers told us they did not consider their card to be a college student credit card, but we counted it as such because the card was expressly labeled and marketed as being for college students.

[21] Since 1996, Student Monitor annually has issued a report on student financial services based on in-person, on-campus interviews of 1,200 undergraduate students enrolled full-time at 100 4-year colleges and universities throughout the United States. According to Student Monitor, the 2013 study had a 2.4 percent margin of error with a 95 percent confidence interval.

[22] We reported the 2000 data from Student Monitor in GAO-01-773, p. 19.

[23] For example, the percentage of students at degree-granting institutions of higher education who were age 25 or older was 43 percent in 2010. GAO analysis of Department of Education, National Center for Education Statistics, NCES 2012-001, *Digest of Education Statistics*, 2011.

[24] Jim Hawkins, "The CARD Act on Campus," *Washington and Lee Law Review*, vol. 69, no. 3 (2012).

[25] Insured commercial banks must submit to their federal regulators (quarterly) a Consolidated Report of Condition and Income, known as a Call Report, which includes a comprehensive balance sheet and income statement, including income generated by credit card portfolios.

[26] CFPB has access to de-identified, account-level information from some issuers; those data are housed with a third-party contractor that provides data warehousing and analytics in the credit card market. However, according to CFPB staff, while some credit card issuers indicate accounts that are student credit cards, comprehensive information specifically on student cardholders is not available. We have ongoing work related to CFPB's data collection and its privacy and security procedures.

[27] Sallie Mae's annual study, which has produced information on college students' credit card use since 2010, uses telephone interviews of a sample of undergraduate students who are 18–24 years old and an unrelated sample of parents of such students. Eight hundred students were interviewed for the 2013 study. The Student Monitor study uses in-person, on-campus interviews of 1,200 college students enrolled full-time at 100 four-year colleges and universities throughout the United States. The firm's *Financial Services* report has included information on student credit card use since 1996. Because the surveys are based on self-reporting of payment behaviors and estimated credit card debt levels, they may be prone to biases and not accurately represent actual behaviors and debt levels. The surveys were not designed to verify that information. Some researchers maintain that respondents sometimes underreport the quantity or level of characteristics that could be considered unflattering, such as the amount of outstanding credit card debt.

[28] Student Monitor, *Financial Services – Spring 2013* (Ridgewood, N.J.: June 2013). Overall credit card ownership includes cards the students own and those for which they have permission to use (typically, parents' cards). The number of students who had a credit card in their name similarly declined—from 46 percent in 2004 to 26 percent in 2013.

[29] Sallie Mae and Ipsos Public Affairs, *How America Pays for College 2013: Sallie Mae's National Study of College Students and Parents* (Newark, Del.: 2013) and Sallie Mae, *How America Pays for College 2010: Sallie Mae's National Study of College Students and Parents Conducted by Gallup* (Reston, Va.: 2010).

[30] Consumer Financial Protection Bureau, *CARD Act Report: A Review of the Impact of the CARD Act on the Consumer Credit Card Market* (Washington D.C.: Oct. 1, 2013). The reported numbers are based on an inquiry conducted by the CFPB Office of Supervision gathering information from a number of large banks on their credit card and CARD Act compliance practices. The issuers that participated in this inquiry represented approximately 80 percent of credit card industry balances.

[31] The data in the analysis were from the New York Federal Reserve Bank Consumer Credit Panel/Equifax. The Consumer Credit Panel contains detailed records of individual debt and borrowing on a quarterly basis from the first quarter of 1999 to the most recent quarter. The study looked at data from 2005-2008 for individuals between 18 and 25 years old. Peter Debbaut, Andra Ghent, and Marianna Kudlyak, *Are Young Borrowers Bad Borrowers? Evidence from the Credit CARD Act of 2009* (Richmond, Va.: July 11, 2013).

[32] See Student Monitor, 2013.

[33] Jesse Bricker, Arthur B. Kennickell, Kevin B. Moore, and John Sabelhaus, "Changes in U.S. Family Finances from 2007 to 2010: Evidence from the Survey of Consumer Finances," *Federal Reserve Bulletin*, vol. 98, no. 2 (June 2012). Additionally, three issuers of college student credit cards told us that those cards' credit limits were typically lower than those of general credit cards.

[34] Student Monitor asked respondents whether they typically carried a balance or paid the card in full each month for four different credit card types and combined the responses. Sallie Mae asked respondents to describe their typical credit card payment behavior.

[35] Debbaut, et al.

End Notes for Appendix I

[1] The Credit Card Accountability Responsibility and Disclosure Act of 2009 required issuers to submit annually to the Federal Reserve the terms and conditions of any college credit card agreement in effect between the issuer and an institution of higher education at any time during the preceding calendar year, along with certain summary information about the agreements. Pub. L. No. 111-24, § 305(a),123 Stat. 1734, 1750; 12 C.F.R. § 1026.57(d). This responsibility transferred from the Federal Reserve to CFPB in 2011. Dodd-Frank Wall Street Reform and Consumer Protection Act, Pub. L. No. 111-203, 124 Stat. 1376 (2010).

[2] For our review, we classified agreements that had been recorded as being with alumni associations or alumni under "alumni associations." We used "other" to include agreements with fraternities, sororities, professional or trade organizations, and those with multiple organizations, such as a university and an alumni association.

[3] The database can be accessed at http://data.consumerfinance.gov/Government/CollegeCredit-Card-Agreements/r963-hvsf. We downloaded the data on December 4, 2012. As of December 2, 2013, the 2011 data remained the most current available.

[4] We combined two companies listed in the database—Capital One Bank (USA), N.A. and Capital One, N.A.—because they are both subsidiaries of Capital One Financial Corporation.

[5] Results from nonprobability samples cannot be used to make inferences about a population, because in a nonprobability sample some elements of a population being studied have no chance or an unknown chance of being selected as part of the sample. We selected our sample from the 574 agreements that were still in effect as of January 1, 2012, instead of the broader set of 798 filed agreements in 2011, because we were most interested in current agreements.

[6] We excluded from our sample agreements with Elevations Credit Union, Pennsylvania State Employees Credit Union, and USC Credit Union because they did not contain credit card products, and we excluded agreements with Compass Bank because they were not with organizations associated with higher education, and therefore were outside the scope of our review.

[7] Sallie Mae's annual study, which has produced information on college students' credit card use since 2010, uses telephone interviews of a sample of undergraduate students 18–24 years old and an unrelated sample of parents of such students. Eight hundred students were interviewed for the 2013 study. The Student Monitor study uses in-person, on-campus interviews of 1,200 college students enrolled full-time at 100 colleges and universities throughout the United States. The firm's Financial Services report has included information on student credit card use since 1996.

[8] Pub. L. No. 111-24, §§ 301-305, 123 Stat. 1734,1747-51.

[9] *The Nilson Report* is a twice-monthly trade journal that provides information on companies, products, and services from the payments industry.

In: College Credit and Debit Cards
Editor: Evalyn Linette Trent
ISBN: 978-1-63321-116-2

Chapter 2

COLLEGE DEBIT CARDS: ACTIONS NEEDED TO ADDRESS ATM ACCESS, STUDENT CHOICE, AND TRANSPARENCY*

United States Government Accountability Office

WHY GAO DID THIS STUDY

A growing number of colleges and universities have entered into agreements with financial firms to provide debit and prepaid card services for students. As the number of agreements has grown, questions have arisen over fees and issues such as student choice. This chapter examines (1) the functions of college cards and the characteristics of schools and card providers offering the cards; and (2) benefits and concerns regarding these cards. GAO reviewed relevant federal laws and regulations, developed a tally of card agreements by reviewing industry reports and school and provider websites, and analyzed data and interviewed officials from federal agencies, banks and other financial firms, students, and industry and consumer groups. GAO selected nine schools (which vary by program length and sector) for extended interviews and data collection.

* This is an edited, reformatted and augmented version of the United States Government Accountability Office publication, GAO-14-91, dated February 2014.

What GAO Recommends

Congress should consider requiring that financial firms providing debit and prepaid card services to colleges file their agreements for public review and provide other relevant information. The Department of Education should (1) specify what constitutes convenient access to ATMs or bank branch offices for students receiving federal student aid funds and (2) develop requirements for schools and card providers to present neutral information to students about their options for receiving federal student aid funds. The Bureau of Consumer Financial Protection agreed with GAO's matter for Congress. Education agreed with GAO's recommendations to it and said it will address these issues in an upcoming process to develop new rules.

What GAO Found

At least 852 schools, or 11 percent of U.S. colleges and universities, had agreements to provide debit or prepaid card services to their students as of July 2013, and most offered students the ability to receive federal student aid and other payments on a card. These schools were disproportionately large; their enrollments constituted about 40 percent of all postsecondary students. However, the percentage of students enrolled in their schools' college card programs was unknown. In the majority of agreements, the schools also outsourced to their card provider the process for paying financial aid and other funds via college cards and other methods. Some schools also used college cards as student identification. The dominant provider was Higher One, a nonbank financial firm that had a 57 percent market share in 2013, as measured by number of card agreements.

Benefits of college cards can include convenience for students and cost savings and efficiencies for schools, but concerns exist in a number of areas:

- **Fees**. GAO found that fees charged by college card providers generally were comparable with those for similar products provided by banks, although some college card fees were slightly higher than those of credit unions. However, two large providers charged a fee for card purchases using a personal identification number (PIN) rather than a signature—a fee mainstream debit cards typically do not charge. The total fees students pay are not known, and some providers declined or said they were unable to provide these data to GAO. In 2012, Higher One settled with the Federal Deposit Insurance Corporation, which alleged unfair and deceptive practices that resulted in consumers paying higher fees.

- **ATM access.** Officials at nine selected schools generally did not report significant issues with the availability of fee-free automated teller machines (ATM) on campus. Although Department of Education regulations for college cards require that schools ensure "convenient access" to fee-free ATMs or bank branches for students receiving federal student aid payments, the agency has not specified what constitutes this level of access. The lack of a more specific definition may make avoiding unnecessary fees difficult for students when making cash withdrawals of federal aid.
- **Neutrality.** GAO found instances in which schools or card providers appeared to encourage students to enroll in a college card rather than present neutral information about payment options. The financial marketplace functions best when consumers are fully informed and have unbiased information. However, schools may have incentives to influence student choice because some receive payments from card providers based on the number of card accounts or transactions, leading some consumer advocates to question whether schools always act in their students' best interests. Furthermore, the contracts between schools and card providers are not publicly available and data on these cards are limited, in contrast to another college-related product—affinity credit cards bearing the institution's name or logo—for which key information must be disclosed. Increased transparency for college card agreements could help ensure that the terms are fair and reasonable for students and the agreements are free from conflicts of interest.

ABBREVIATIONS

ATM	automated teller machine
CFPB	Bureau of Consumer Financial Protection
EBT	electronic benefit transfer
FDIC	Federal Deposit Insurance Corporation
FERPA	Family Educational Rights and Privacy Act
FTC	Federal Trade Commission

IPEDS	Integrated Postsecondary Education Data System
NACUBO	National Association of College and University Business Officers
PIN	personal identification number
PIRG	U.S. Public Interest Research Group
SNAP	Supplemental Nutrition Assistance Program
TANF	Temporary Assistance for Needy Families
WIC	Special Supplemental Nutrition Program for Women, Infants, and Children

February 13, 2014

The Honorable Tom Harkin
Chairman
Committee on Health, Education, Labor, and Pensions
United States Senate

Dear Mr. Chairman:

In recent years, a growing number of schools have begun offering banking products to their students in the form of debit and prepaid cards issued through agreements with financial services providers. These college cards provide students with debit or checking account services, but also can serve as student identification cards or be used to deliver student aid. Some federal agencies, consumer advocacy groups, and members of Congress have raised concerns over issues associated with college cards, such as the fees students can incur, including when accessing federal student aid. In fiscal year 2012, the Department of Education (Education) administered federal student aid programs that provided about $142 billion in grants and loans to 15 million students.[1]

In this report, we review issues related to college debit and prepaid card agreements, examining (1) the functions of college cards and the characteristics of schools and card providers offering the cards, and (2) benefits and concerns regarding these cards. To characterize the college card marketplace and examine issues surrounding use of the cards, we reviewed relevant federal laws and regulations and documentation from federal agencies, including Education, the Federal Deposit Insurance Corporation (FDIC), the Bureau of Consumer Financial Protection (also known as CFPB), and the Board of Governors of the Federal Reserve System (Federal Reserve).

We also interviewed representatives of these agencies. We collected and analyzed information on schools' agreements with college card providers and developed a tally of current card agreements by reviewing industry reports, interviewing college card providers, and obtaining information from school and provider websites.

We also used data from Education's Integrated Postsecondary Education Data System (IPEDS) to analyze the student and institutional characteristics of these schools and compare them with the overall college and university population. We assessed the reliability of the IPEDS data by reviewing documentation about the systems used to produce the data and considering our previous use of the data, and we determined that the data were sufficiently reliable for our reporting purposes.

We selected nine institutions with college card agreements for extended interviews and data collection. We selected this nongeneralizable sample by focusing on schools with larger enrollments and higher proportions of students receiving federal student loans, and included a mix of school types (2- and 4-year, public, nonprofit, and for-profit) and geographic locations.[2] We examined online and paper materials provided to students at these nine schools, and we reviewed card agreements from five of them, representing about 51 percent of the student population at the nine schools. We interviewed student government leaders at five of these schools where we could arrange meetings with students. In addition, we interviewed representatives of eight banks and financial firms that are the largest providers of college cards, composing about 90 percent of the market we identified. We reviewed college card contracts and other publicly available information on cardholder fees for these eight providers. For comparison purposes, we reviewed information on fees for similar checking accounts from five other large national banks and average credit union account fees published by the Credit Union National Association. We reviewed documentation from other federal programs that distribute benefits electronically on cards, including those administered by the Departments of Labor, Agriculture, Health and Human Services, and the Treasury. We also interviewed industry executives and consumer advocates. See appendix I for a detailed discussion of our scope and methodology.

We conducted this performance audit from November 2012 to February 2014 in accordance with generally accepted government auditing standards. Those standards require that we plan and perform the audit to obtain sufficient, appropriate evidence to provide a reasonable basis for our findings and conclusions based on our audit objectives. We believe that the evidence obtained provides a reasonable basis for our findings and conclusions based on our audit objectives.

Background

Schools with college card agreements generally provide students with access to either a debit or prepaid card. Each type of card offers a cashless means to make purchases and access funds, but there are key differences between them.[3]

- A debit card is issued by a bank and linked to a customer's checking account. It allows the customer to withdraw cash from the account or to pay for goods and services. In a debit transaction, the amount of the transaction is withdrawn from the available balance in the cardholder's account.
- Prepaid cards appear and function much like a debit card, but are not linked to an individual consumer's bank account.[4] Instead, an amount is deposited into a pooled account, and withdrawals or purchases are made against the predeposited amount. Prepaid cards can be single-use or reloadable. Both banks and nonbank financial firms issue prepaid cards, but banks issue the majority of them, according to FDIC.

Schools can use college cards to make payments to students, such as financial aid or tuition refunds when a student withdraws from a class.[5] The majority of financial aid is provided by federal student loan and grant programs, although students also can obtain aid from states, school grants, and other sources. Federal student aid can be used to pay for tuition and fees, room and board, books, supplies, and other living expenses. The aid is generally paid directly to the school, which deducts its charges, such as tuition and fees. If a student's total payments from all sources, including financial aid, exceed the school's charges, the school pays the difference (also known as a credit balance or credit balance refund) to the student. The bulk of the funds paid to students may be federal student aid remaining after paying for tuition and fees, and the money is intended to help students pay for nonschool items related to their education, such as living expenses and transportation costs. Figure 1 depicts the process for paying financial aid and other funds to students.

Schools can manage these payments themselves or contract with a third party to administer the process.

When a school pays federal student aid funds to a student, the process is subject to Department of Education requirements, which are aimed at ensuring that students receive the funds in a timely and effective manner.[6] For example, Education requires schools to pay any federal student aid funds that exceed the school's charges directly to students as soon as possible, but no later than 14 days after the first day of classes or the date the funds were posted to the student's account (whichever occurs later). Schools must pay these funds to students in cash or by check or electronic transfer to either a bank account, a checking account that can be accessed by a debit card, or a prepaid card.

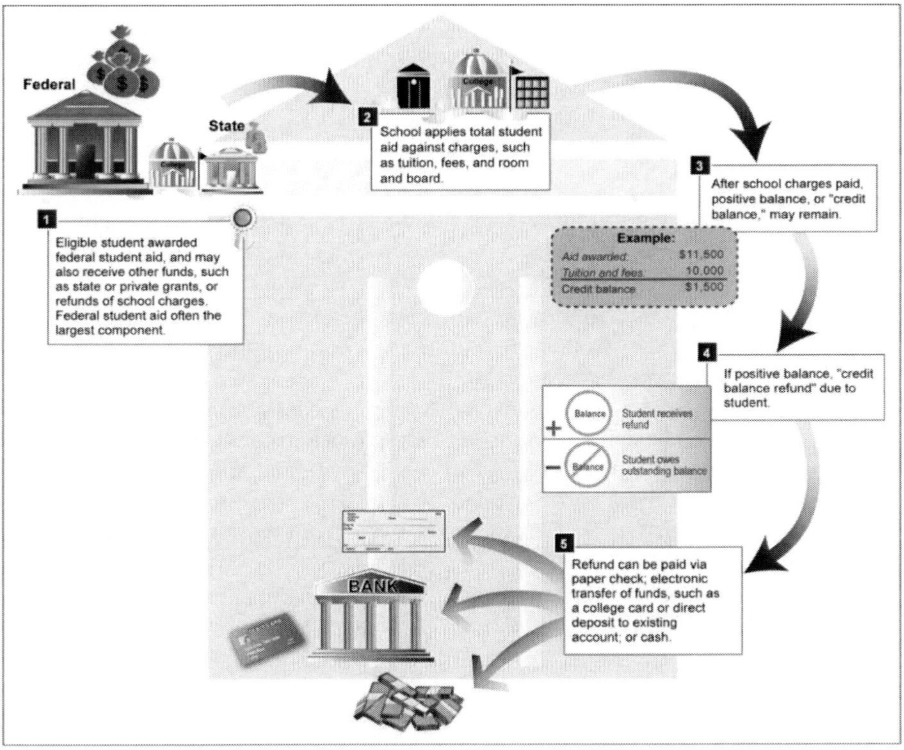

Source: GAO analysis of Education guidance.

Figure 1. Overview of Process for Paying Financial Aid and Other Funds to Students.

Table 1. Selected Requirements of Department of Education for Use of Debit and Prepaid Cards

Feature or characteristic	Guidance/requirement for school
Student consent	Schools must obtain consent from student or parent to open a bank account or load funds onto a prepaid card. If student does not consent to receiving funds on a debit or prepaid card, school must pay the student by cash, check, or electronic transfer to the student's bank account.
Notifications	Before the student account is opened, schools must inform students of terms and conditions of the account or prepaid card, including fees and other costs.
Protections	Funds must be held in an insured account (by the Federal Deposit Insurance Corporation or National Credit Union Share Insurance Fund). Debit or prepaid cards cannot be marketed or portrayed as credit cards and cannot subsequently be converted to credit cards.
Prohibited fees	Schools must ensure students or parents do not incur costs when opening accounts or initially receiving debit or prepaid cards to access federal student aid funds.
Access to funds	Debit and prepaid cards must be convertible to cash and widely usable (institution may not limit use of cards to particular vendors). Students must have convenient access on (or "immediately adjacent" to) campus to branch offices or automated teller machines (ATM) of the banks or financial firms with which accounts were opened, so that students do not incur fees when making cash withdrawals from those offices or ATMs.

Source: GAO analysis of federal regulations.

Note: In particular, see 34 C.F.R. 668.164(c)(2)-(3); Department of Education, Office of Postsecondary Education, *Responses to Recent, Recurring Federal Student Aid Questions*, "Dear Colleague" Letter GEN-05-16 (Oct. 27, 2005).

Furthermore, schools that use debit and prepaid cards to pay federal student aid funds must follow additional requirements. As shown in table 1, Education's requirements focus on ensuring that students have free access to federal student aid and are not forced to use a particular debit or prepaid card. And if schools contract with a bank or financial firm to manage the payment of federal aid to students, Education requires schools to ensure that the contractors comply with applicable regulations and provisions for federal aid.

Education also encourages, but does not require, schools to annually disclose a breakdown of the average annual costs their students incur in using college cards.[7]

In addition to Education's requirements, other federal laws and regulations provide consumer protections applicable to all debit and prepaid cards. For example, Section 5 of the Federal Trade Commission Act prohibits unfair or deceptive acts or practices.[8] The act applies to banks, as they are engaged in interstate commerce, and federal banking agencies have authority to enforce Section 5 against entities they supervise. CFPB has authority to enforce prohibitions on unfair and abusive acts against certain institutions and service providers. Regulation E, which implements the Electronic Fund Transfer Act, includes disclosure requirements and limits on cardholder liability for debit cards (but not prepaid cards).[9] (For more information on federal protections for debit and prepaid card users, see app. IV.) CFPB has authority to enforce the Electronic Fund Transfer Act and certain other federal consumer financial laws against certain institutions and service providers, while ensuring that consumers can access financial products and services.[10] CFPB also can issue rules and examine certain institutions.

College Cards Are Used for Multiple Purposes and Are Offered by at Least 852 Schools

College cards offer a range of financial services to students, including delivering financial aid and making other payments. Of about 7,600 colleges and universities participating in federal student aid programs, we found 852 (11 percent) had college card agreements.[11] Because these schools were generally larger, their student populations represented about 40 percent of total enrollment. However, even when schools have college card agreements, not all students participate in their school's card program. One provider, Higher One, had more than half the market for college cards.

College Cards Can Be Used for Several Functions

College cards can be used for different functions, which vary depending on the school and the provider:

Financial services. About 80 percent of college card agreements we identified were for debit cards, with the remainder for prepaid cards.[12] The cards can provide the same functions of standard debit or prepaid cards, which include the ability to withdraw funds from an ATM and make purchases in stores and online. Debit cards link to a standard bank account, with check-writing capability and access to services at the bank's branch locations.

Paying Financial Aid and Other Funds to Students. College debit and prepaid cards can be used to deliver federal student aid or make other payments. As part of its card agreement, the school can contract with the card provider to administer the student payment process on the school's behalf. Generally, students can elect to have their funds deposited to the account associated with their college card, or they can choose to receive their funds by direct deposit to another account or in cash or by paper check. More than 80 percent of the schools we identified with card agreements indicated that students could use their cards to receive financial aid and other funds from the school.[13] By school sector, this included 88 percent of public schools with card agreements, 70 percent of nonprofit schools, and 100 percent of for-profit schools. (See app. II for a discussion of other federal programs that use prepaid or electronic benefit cards to provide payments to beneficiaries.)

Student ID card. In one-third of schools we identified with card agreements, the student's ID also can be used to access banking services. In these cases, either the school or the card provider issues student ID cards to all students. Students then can choose whether to have their ID card also serve as a debit or prepaid card.

At Least 852 Schools, Including Many Large Public Colleges, Have College Card Agreements

In our review of industry reports and school and provider websites, and our interviews with card providers, we identified 852 U.S. colleges and universities with college card agreements as of July 2013, representing about 11 percent of all schools participating in federal student aid programs.[14] However, schools that have adopted college cards were disproportionately large—the enrollment at these schools represented about 39 percent of all students at schools participating in federal student aid programs (see Figure 2). In particular, 12 of the 20 largest schools by enrollment had college card agreements.[15]

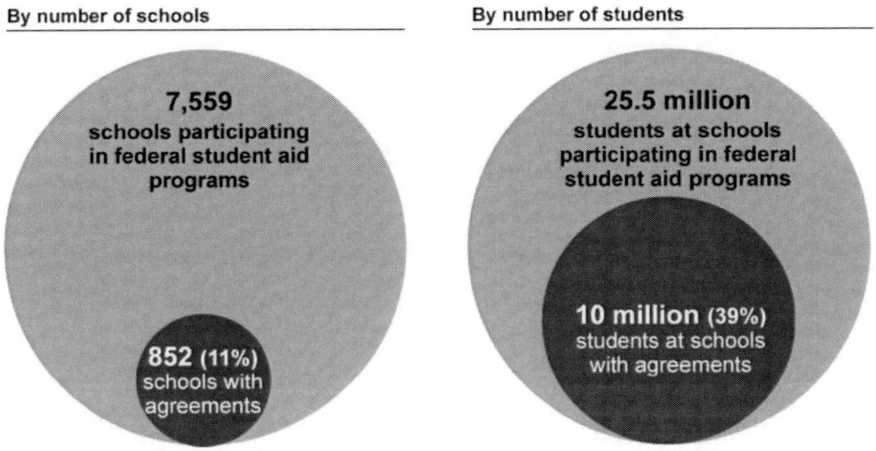

Sources: GAO analysis of Education data, industry reports, and school and provider information.

Figure 2. Prevalence of College Card Agreements by Number of Schools and Number of Students, as of July 2013.

We found card agreements were most common at public colleges and universities. About 29 percent of public schools had card agreements, compared with 6.5 percent of nonprofit schools and 3.5 percent of for- profit schools. In each school sector, 4-year schools also were more likely to have agreements than 2-year or less than 2-year schools (see Figure 3). For the student characteristics of age, race, and financial aid status, we found that schools with college card agreements generally were similar to schools without agreements.[16]

Comprehensive data are not available on how many students choose to enroll in a college card. We found a range of adoption rates among schools and providers we interviewed. For example, the largest provider reported that overall, 43 percent of students receiving financial aid payments at its client schools opened debit accounts. However, the adoption rate varied considerably by school–for example, 20 percent of participating students at one school with which we spoke opted to open accounts, compared with 75 percent at another school. At some schools, officials told us that only students who were expected to receive payments were offered cards.[17] Conversely, other school officials told us that all students received cards, but students might be less likely to activate cards if they did not believe they would receive a payment from the school.

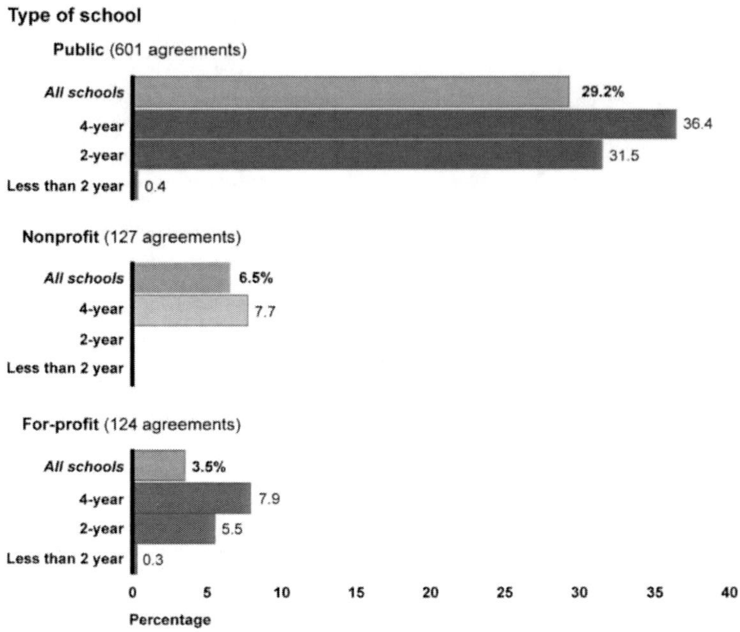

Sources: GAO analysis of Education data, industry reports, and school and provider information.

Figure 3. Percentage of Schools with College Card Agreements, by Sector and Program Length, as of July 2013.

Our analysis showed that public 2-year schools, or community colleges, represented almost half of all schools that used college cards to make financial aid and other payments to students. According to the National Association of College and University Business Officers (NACUBO), community college students are among those more likely to receive a financial aid payment because they generally have low tuition and fees to deduct from students' available financial aid funds. In turn, according to NACUBO, community college students are more likely to obtain funds through a college card than other students.

One Nonbank Financial Firm Had More Than Half of the College Card Market

As of July 2013, one provider, Higher One Holdings, Inc., held about a 57 percent share of the college card market, as measured by number of agreements between schools and card providers, as well as number of students at schools with agreements, according to our analysis. Seven other providers, which included bank and nonbank providers, represented most of the rest of the market (see Figure 4).[18]

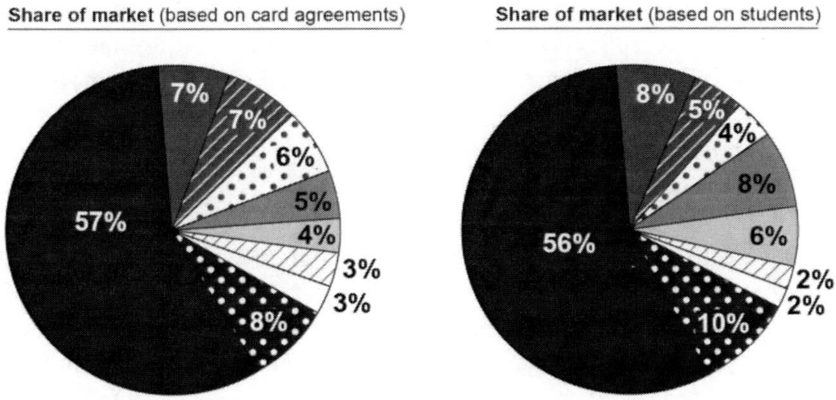

Card provider	Provider type	Service: Debit	Service: Prepaid	Service: Financial aid and other student payments
Higher One	Nonbank	✓	☐	✓
U.S. Bank	Bank	✓	✓	✓
Sallie Mae[a]	Nonbank	☐	✓	✓
PNC	Bank	✓	✓	✓
Wells Fargo	Bank	✓	☐	✓
Citibank	Bank	☐	✓	✓
Heartland	Nonbank	☐	✓	✓
Blackboard	Nonbank	☐	✓	✓
Other	Various	✓	✓	✓

Sources: GAO analysis of Education data, industry reports, and school and provider information.

[a] In May 2013, Higher One announced the acquisition of Sallie Mae's Campus Solutions business, which includes college card operations.

Figure 4. College Card Providers, by Provider Type, Type of Card Offered, and Market Share, as of July 2013.

Higher One, founded in 2000, is a nonbank financial firm that contracts with banks to perform the banking functions associated with its college cards, which include providing checking accounts, processing wire transfers, supplying cash for ATMs, and issuing cards. Higher One provides processing and other administrative services, including managing customer service, and is responsible for the information technology for managing the accounts. For 2012, Higher One reported net income of $36.9 million on revenue of $197.7 million, with average annual net income growth of 37 percent over the previous 3 years. Seventy-six percent of its 2012 revenue derived from accounts opened by students and other members of the campus community, including accountholder fees and interchange fees.[19] Company executives have said that interchange revenue accounted for between 40 and 50 percent of account revenue through the first three quarters of 2013. The company's other sources of revenue include managing financial aid and other student payments for schools, and providing students and parents with other financial services. In addition, Higher One receives fees from its bank partners based in part on the amount of deposits in student accounts that these banks hold. In May 2013, Higher One announced it acquired the college card operations of Sallie Mae, which represented about 7 percent of the college card market as measured by the number of schools with agreements. While Higher One's main business is college cards, it also has been expanding into other school-related areas, such as student data analytics.[20]

The six other providers of college cards among the group of eight we identified are:

- **U.S. Bank, PNC Bank, Wells Fargo Bank, and Citibank**—large banks that provide college card services among a number of other financial products.
- **Blackboard, Inc.**—an education technology and services company, whose other products include online learning, campus commerce and security, and school communication.
- **Heartland Payment Systems, Inc.**—a payments processing firm, active in credit, debit, and prepaid card processing, which has expanded into the college card marketplace.

Like Higher One, Blackboard and Heartland use bank partners. Higher One and some other providers said they have been seeking to expand the number of schools with which they have college card agreements. Some of the companies also noted they have been expanding their offerings—for example, by adding the option of prepaid cards in addition to debit cards, or by offering to administer a school's process for making financial aid and other student payments.

College Cards Can Benefit Students and Schools, but Concerns Exist about Fees, Student Choice, and Transparency

Benefits of college cards can include administrative savings for schools and added convenience of use for students. In general, college card fees were not higher than those associated with other banking products available to students. The largest card provider's practices in charging fees, however, were the subject of an FDIC enforcement action in 2012, which resulted in a settlement without admission of a violation of law. In addition, other concerns with college cards include students' access to no-fee ATMs, schools' influence over students' banking and payment choices, potential conflicts of interest for schools, and the lack of transparency surrounding card agreements.

Benefits of College Cards Include Reducing School Costs and Offering Students Banking Options

School officials and college card providers cited several benefits to schools of entering into college card agreements:

- **Electronic payment of funds.** Several schools told us they contracted with a college card provider primarily because they wanted to reduce expenses by paying funds electronically rather than by paper check, or to avoid the expense of developing an electronic system internally. Processing paper checks is costly and labor- intensive, according to school officials, with one school official estimating that it cost upwards of $25 to issue a paper check. Paper checks are also vulnerable to fraud because they can be altered or stolen.
- **Lower administrative costs.** Even if schools have the internal capability to process funds electronically, college card providers can do so more cheaply, or at no expense to the school, according to card providers and some schools. Although card providers may charge

schools for student payment services, officials from two schools told us the cost under their card agreements was still less than half what it would be to process the same transactions internally. For example, officials at one school estimated the school saved about $0.75 on each check and $0.15 on each direct deposit by contracting with a provider. These small per-transaction differences can produce significant savings for schools administering many transactions each year. At one of the six schools we reviewed that contracted with a card provider to manage student payments, the card provider administered the process at no cost to the school.[21]

- **Improved student ID cards.** College cards can allow schools to expand the functionality, or defray the cost, of their student ID cards. For example, one school said the electronic building access provided by its college card improved security because the previous ID card could be altered easily and students were able to access buildings simply by showing the card. One college card provider also said it has helped schools defray the cost of student ID programs by providing free card stock for printing the ID cards.
- **Revenue generation.** As discussed later in this report, some college card agreements include payments from card providers to schools—for example, based on student account activity—or provide other benefits, such as administering student payments for schools at nominal rates.
- **Reduced use of cash on campus.** Some schools prefer the use of college cards at the campus bookstore and other campus locations because they find card transactions cheaper and more convenient to manage than cash transactions, according to one card provider.

College cards also can benefit students, according to students, school officials, and card providers we interviewed. Benefits they cited include the following:

- **Access to banking services.** College cards provide a way to enter the mainstream banking system for students who do not have bank accounts. Evidence suggests that some college students are unbanked—that is, they do not have any kind of bank or other deposit account at an insured depository institution.[22] These students may rely on alternative financial providers, such as check cashing services and payday lenders, that have higher costs and lack consumer protections available with a traditional bank account. For example, officials at one school estimated that about 300 of their nearly 15,000 students were unable to get a traditional bank account.[23]

- **Multipurpose convenience.** When banking services are linked to a student ID card, students may benefit from using a single card for school and banking functions, such as campus building access, library book checkout, ATM use, or purchases.
- **Quicker access to funds.** When schools outsource the process for making financial aid and other payments to a card provider, students can get their funds faster, according to card providers and schools. Card providers and school officials told us that funds are usually available on college cards the same day the school releases funds to the provider, compared with availability in 2-3 business days for direct deposit to another account, or 5-7 business days for a paper check.[24] Students generally want to get their funds as quickly as possible, according to students and school officials we interviewed, because they can face large expenses at the beginning of a term for rent, textbooks, and other college costs.
- **Financial education.** Some college card providers offer financial education and budget tools that can help students manage their finances. For example, officials at one school said their college card provider offered on-campus financial education sessions for students, while officials at another school noted their card provider gave students online breakdowns of their spending. One provider has given grants for on-campus financial literacy efforts.[25]

Most College Card Fees Are Comparable to Similar Bank Products; PIN Fees and ATM Access Are Concerns and Total Fees Paid Are Unknown

Fees Generally Comparable to Those Other Institutions Charge, Except for PIN Transactions

Most of the college card fees we reviewed generally were not higher, or in some cases were lower, than those associated with a selection of basic or student checking accounts at national banks.[26] In particular, college card accounts generally did not have monthly maintenance fees, while the basic checking accounts we reviewed typically did (see table 2). College card fees for out-of-network ATM use, wire transfers, and overdrafts also were generally comparable with those of banks' basic and student checking accounts. However, fees charged by credit unions typically were the same or lower than those charged by college cards. In addition, college card fees are likely lower than those of alternative financial services, such as check-cashing services, that some students without bank accounts might otherwise use.[27] See appendix III for more detailed information on our fee comparison analysis.

One area where college card fees can exceed those of traditional bank accounts is for purchases made using a personal identification number (PIN). Two college card providers—Higher One and Citibank, which together represent about 60 percent of the market—charge $0.50 for transactions that use PINs rather than signatures.[28] No basic or student account that we reviewed for comparison purposes charged a transaction fee for using the account's debit card. Approximately one-third of all PIN transactions are for less than $15, according to the Federal Reserve, which can make a $0.50 fee a significant cost relative to the amount of the transaction. While students can avoid the fee by authorizing their purchase using a signature rather than a PIN, the signature option involves using a keypad option labeled "credit," which may be confusing because the card is a debit card and not a credit card.[29] In addition, CFPB staff told us that some merchants make selecting the credit option more difficult, because debit transactions offer them more favorable interchange fees.

Some federal officials and students have expressed concerns that college card fees are too high. In 2012, as part of its process to consider new regulations on debit cards, Education received some comments criticizing college card fees for being too high, unnecessary, and reducing the amount of student aid available to cover college costs.[30] Some public comments submitted by students to CFPB in 2013 also complained about high fees, including the PIN debit transaction charge.[31] CFPB staff similarly told us that while college cards in some cases had higher fees than other products, they did not appear to offer any more attractive features.

Out-of-Network Fees and ATM Access Have Been Raised as Issues

Consumer advocates and federal officials also have expressed concerns about the extent to which students incur out-of-network ATM charges when using their college cards and their ability to access fee-free ATMs. As is typical for debit cards in general, all the college card providers we reviewed charged no fee for withdrawals from ATMs within that card's network. Providers have charged fees up to $3.00 for withdrawals from out-of-network ATMs, with the majority charging $2.50.[32] Additionally, operators of the out-of-network ATMs may impose a surcharge of their own, which is typically about $2.00.[33] One card provider noted that these ATM fees can add up, because many college students make frequent ATM withdrawals of small sums.

The number of in-network, fee-free ATMs available to students with college cards varies significantly depending on the school and the card provider. Our review of nine schools illustrated this variation: one large school had 16 in-network ATMs on one campus, while a smaller school had one.[34] Five of the providers we reviewed also had contracts with ATM networks other than their own to provide additional fee-free access to students. However, at least one of these providers—Higher One—only provides students access to its broader fee-free ATM network if they open an account with a monthly maintenance fee, potentially reducing any savings realized through the improved ATM access.[35]

A 2012 report by the U.S. Public Interest Research Group (PIRG), a consumer advocacy organization, also asserted that at some schools, students may experience lengthy lines at college card ATMs or have limited access to ATMs in school buildings that are not open 24 hours a day. Officials at eight of the nine schools with whom we spoke generally did not indicate that access to in-network ATMs was a significant or widespread issue. One school acknowledged that sometimes lines of 20-40 students formed at the ATM on the first day that funds were paid to student accounts. We also found that for one large provider, 5 percent of its ATMs were accessible 24 hours a day; however, the provider noted that it does not control the hours of the buildings in which the ATMs are located.

Education regulations for delivering federal student aid funds on college cards require that schools ensure students have "convenient access" to ATMs or a branch office where students will not incur any costs making cash withdrawals from the bank in which the account was opened.[36] However, Education has provided a limited definition of what constitutes such access—namely, that the branch office or ATMs must be located on the institution's campus, in institutionally owned or operated facilities, or a location immediately adjacent to and accessible from the campus.[37] Although this definition provides some guidance, it does not take account of such factors as actual ATM usage patterns or availability. Education staff said that a better definition or more specific standards for convenient access to fee-free ATMs may be needed, noting concerns that a single on-campus ATM may not be sufficient and could result in students incurring unnecessary fees. The department announced its intention to develop new regulations for college cards in a May 2012 notice, but staff told us they had been focusing on other regulatory priorities.[38] However, in November 2013 Education announced formation of a committee to develop proposed regulations on college cards and other issues, with the committee scheduled to begin work in February 2014.[39] Any new regulations may address the issue of ATM access and fees, Education staff told us.

Table 2. Comparison of Selected Account Fees, by Provider Type, as of August- September 2013

Fee	College cards	Large banks, general checking accounts	Credit unions (median fees)[a]
Monthly maintenance 	$0[b]	Standard account: $6-$12 Student account: $0-$5	$0
Out-of-network ATM transaction 	$2-$3	$2-$2.50	$1
PIN (personal identification number) transaction 	$0-$0.50	$0	$0
Overdraft[c] 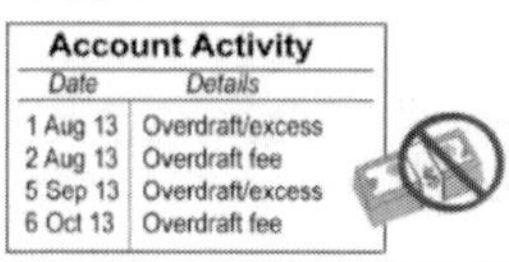	$29-$36	$34-$36	$25
Outgoing wire transfer 	$25-$30	$24-$30	$15

Source: GAO analysis of provider information.

[a] Based on survey responses from 1,100 credit unions. Median fee amounts are based on credit unions that charged a particular fee. When the majority of credit unions

did not charge a specific fee, the median amount is reported as $0. See Credit Union National Association, 2013-2014 Fees Report. Fee information on outgoing wire transfers is from the Credit Union National Association's 2011-2012 fees report because this fee information was not reported in the 2013-2014 report.

[b] Higher One's basic account has no monthly fee. The company also offers students two other account options, which charge monthly fees of up to $5.95 but, among other things, do not charge PIN fees or fees on certain ATM withdrawals. Sallie Mae also had charged a $4.95 monthly maintenance fee for its prepaid college card but sold its student card operations to Higher One in 2013. PNC also changes a $5 monthly fee for its prepaid college card, but this card is only offered at two institutions. PNC does not charge students a monthly maintenance fee for its more common debit college cards.

[c] According to the Federal Reserve, an overdraft for a debit card account can occur when an accountholder writes a check or makes an automatic bill payment or other electronic payment for an amount greater than the balance in the account.

Data Unavailable on Total Fees Paid

Although college card fee schedules we reviewed generally were not higher than those of basic or student checking accounts, little information is available on the frequency with which students incur ATM, PIN, and other fees, and the total amount of college card fees paid by students is unknown. Several college card providers with which we spoke generally were unwilling or unable to provide details or a breakout of their fee revenues.[40] However, one provider with a smaller share of the college card market told us that in the specific case of student financial aid payments, its experience was that students used 82 percent of such funds without incurring fees. Although Education encourages schools to disclose annually a breakdown of the average yearly costs incurred by their students for using their college cards, none of the schools with which we spoke tracked such costs. According to FDIC staff, some students have complained of paying aggregate fees ranging from hundreds of dollars to more than $1,000, but it is unknown whether such fee amounts are typical.

Moreover, college card providers and school officials noted that students can limit fees by adjusting their behavior. For example, students can avoid fees in some cases by choosing to authorize debit transactions using a signature rather than a PIN, or by avoiding withdrawals from out- of-network ATMs. Card providers and schools also told us that they help students avoid card-related fees, such as by e-mailing alerts when account balances are running low or encouraging students to avoid PIN- based debit transactions. However, there are limitations to any efforts to help individuals improve their financial behaviors. Even when given appropriate information, consumers may not make the most rational financial choices. Behaviors such as procrastination and inertia can mitigate against informed choice.[41]

Recently, the largest college card provider faced an administrative enforcement action for its fee-charging practices. In August 2012, FDIC announced settlements with Higher One and a former bank partner, The Bancorp Bank, for alleged unfair and deceptive practices related to how Higher One charged fees for its student debit card account program, among other things.[42] The settlement required Higher One to change its practices for charging fees (for example, limiting the number of insufficient funds fees charged on a single day to a single account) and pay restitution of about $11 million to approximately 60,000 students.[43] FDIC also imposed civil money penalties of $110,000 on Higher One.[44] FDIC staff told us the restitution payments were made and that the agency continues to monitor Higher One's compliance with the consent order. Neither Higher One nor The Bancorp Bank admitted to a violation of law in settling the charges.

In addition, Higher One announced in November 2013 that it reached an agreement in principle to settle a class action lawsuit for $15 million.[45] The company and two of its business partners were named as defendants, with students alleging that Higher One misled students by marketing its debit card as schools' preferred method for making financial aid and other payments, improperly steered them into depositing funds into Higher One accounts, and charged excessive and inadequately disclosed ATM and PIN fees. Higher One and the other defendants denied that marketing of the Higher One account was deceptive and contended that fees were fully disclosed and agreed to by the plaintiffs.

Students May Not Be Offered Neutral Options; Agreements Could Pose Conflicts and Are Not Always Transparent

Concerns have arisen over some school and industry practices that can influence student options, especially when a college card is not necessarily the best option for all students. One issue is whether students' choice to use a college card is unduly influenced by the nature of information they receive about the cards. Another is the extent to which schools' decisions to enter into agreements may be motivated by benefits the schools receive, rather than the best interests of students. However, it is difficult for students and others to assess the influence of financial incentives on school behavior due to the lack of transparency for card agreements. Federal agencies have been reviewing these and other college card issues and may take further action.

College Cards May Not Be the Best Option for All Students

According to some school officials and others we interviewed, college cards may not be the best product for some students who enter college with an existing checking account, or for those who need more comprehensive banking services. Students with both a college card and a separate account with another bank may find it costly or inconvenient to manage both accounts concurrently. For example, officials at one school told us that some students with existing bank accounts who choose to open a separate college card account can incur fees transferring the funds between accounts.

Some college card products also provide less robust banking services and features than a traditional bank account. At its September 2013 forum on financial products marketed to college students, CFPB noted that some student checking products offered by unaffiliated financial institutions have more attractive options than some college cards, such as automatic reimbursement of any ATM fee charged by an out-of-network ATM operator. Prepaid cards in particular may be limited because they may not offer students the ability to write checks, can charge fees for making additional deposits, and provide limited access to a full-service financial institution. Even full-featured college debit cards can have limitations, such as the lack of conveniently located bank branch locations near a student's school or home and unresponsive customer service, both of which were cited in public comments received by CFPB.

Presentation of Card and Payment Options Was Not Always Neutral, Raising Questions about Student Choice

Although schools cannot require students to use college cards, federal officials and consumer advocates have raised concerns about the extent to which students have been able to make fully informed choices about whether to enroll in the debit or prepaid cards their schools offer. Schools and college card providers can affect student choices in several ways:

- **School endorsement.** Schools can appear to implicitly or explicitly endorse their college cards, by virtue of the relationship with the provider and co-branding of the card. Many students trust their schools and, as a result, may view co-branding as an endorsement and an indication their school has negotiated the best terms for them. Education staff said anecdotal evidence supports that idea, noting that students are more likely to sign up for an account when the debit and ID functions are on a single card. Student leaders at four schools with whom we spoke noted that such co-branding—such as a school picture on cards or provider ATMs on campus—gave the appearance of an endorsement by the school or the impression that there is only a single provider.

- **Exclusivity.** Provisions in card contracts that prohibit other financial companies from providing services to students on campus can limit student choice. Four of the eight card providers with which we spoke said that at least some of their agreements with schools include such provisions, such as barring other financial services companies from locating ATMs or an office on campus or from setting up information tables during student orientation.[46]
- **Marketing.** Card providers and schools market college cards directly to students through various methods, including mailings, on-campus presentations, and co-branded websites. Some card providers offer marketing assistance or materials to schools. For example, one provider told us it prefers assisting the school in developing messages, because students pay more attention to the information if it comes from the schools. Some contracts also call for schools to use "best efforts" to promote and encourage use of the provider's account.[47]

Our review of marketing materials and other information offered to students found variations in the type of information provided to students about their financial options. At some schools, students were presented with an unbiased presentation of these options. For example, one school emphasized that "you have the ability to select the option that is best for you," followed by a factual description of payment options. Some schools also recommended direct deposit over their campus card. However, we also identified instances in which payment options were not presented to students in a clear or neutral fashion, and appeared to encourage students to choose the college card over other options. Among these instances were the following:

- One provider, on a website on which students can select a method to receive financial aid and other payments, displays an option where students can immediately select the provider's account. However, students who want to select other options must work through additional instructions, in which the provider continues to encourage use of its product. While the college card payment option can be selected online, an option for deposit to another account requires a separate and more time-consuming submission of additional documentation. The provider told us this requirement is an antifraud measure, but the industry organization that oversees such payment processing transactions told us deposits to another account can be achieved equally well online.[48]

- One school and its provider, under a website heading of "Why should I use the Card?" told students that it "makes everyday life easier on and off campus." The instructions for receiving funds by paper check were less prominent and described a separate, multistep registration process.
- One school directly recommended its college card over the direct deposit alternative and gave guidance to students who already had selected direct deposit on how to switch to the card option.

In public comments received by CFPB, some students said they felt pressured to sign up for college cards. For example, one student said that signing up was "highly encouraged," both during student orientation and when provider representatives appeared on campus. Another described being pressured by a provider representative even after saying she did not plan to sign up. Had she not researched options, she said, she might have been convinced the provider was the only choice. FDIC staff told us that given current practices, it may seem to some students that they must select the school's college card to receive their funds.

Education guidance on college cards does not currently address the marketing of the cards or the extent to which schools must inform students about financial aid payment options, although schools are required to inform students of the terms and conditions of college cards before an account is opened.[49] CFPB recently issued a consumer advisory, reiterating that schools cannot require a particular bank or card to access funds, and advising students to shop around and use direct deposit to an existing account for receiving funds.[50] FDIC staff also told us that requiring a clear and conspicuous affirmative statement that students have a choice could enhance student awareness of options. In addition, in its best practices recommendations for college cards, NACUBO called for "a fair explanation of services [without] misleading, biased, or aggressive marketing schemes."

Payments to Schools May Create Potential Conflicts of Interest

Revenue-sharing agreements appear to be declining, but concerns remain that the payments and other benefits schools receive from card providers may motivate schools to encourage the use of college cards or potentially choose the arrangement that provides the schools the most revenue rather than one that provides students the best terms, according to federal officials and consumer advocates. These payments from providers to schools are generally either a fixed sum or tied to the number of card accounts or the number of card transactions students make. In addition to direct payments, schools can receive other financial benefits from college card providers, such as rent for ATMs located on campus, general marketing assistance for the school ID card program, or savings on the administrative costs of disbursing financial aid.

We did not identify comprehensive information on the number of schools with college cards that receive such payments. Three card providers with which we spoke did not have revenue-sharing agreements with any of their schools. In our review of nine schools, three had agreements with card providers that included revenue-sharing based in part on transaction activity or the number of students who open card accounts. One school told us that it received $13,000 in 2012, based on $10 for each student who activated the college debit card. Another school received $137,000 in payments from the card provider in 2012, based on a formula that included the total balance of student card accounts and the volume of card transactions with vendors. (Partially offsetting that, however, was $30,000 the school paid the provider for services.) A third school told us it has received an average of about $400,000 annually over the life of its contract, which is based in part on the number of students who opened card accounts.

In addition, some schools—apart from the nine that we reviewed in depth—have more comprehensive agreements with providers for activities or financial services in addition to college cards, which can provide considerably larger revenue to the schools. For example, one large public university has a college card agreement with a national bank that includes activity-based revenue sharing. In 2013, the bank was to pay a royalty of $34 for each active college card account, or a minimum of $1 million annually, according to contract documents.[51] In addition, the school has another agreement with the same bank that provides for $35 million over 25 years for such things as naming rights for a football stadium, advertising, and other sponsorships. Similarly, in 2012, another large public university signed a 15-year deal worth at least $25 million with another national bank, which includes providing banking services to the university, alumni, and staff and faculty, in addition to providing college cards.

Education staff and some card providers said that revenue-sharing agreements for college cards have been declining. Reasons for the decline include the negative public attention the practice has received and the reduced need for providers to offer revenue-sharing as an inducement, they said. For example, Higher One recently stated that it discontinued revenue-sharing incentives to new customers in November 2007 and has sought to terminate such provisions in existing agreements. As of March 2013, about 5 percent of Higher One's card contracts with schools contained revenue-sharing provisions, which in 2012 paid an average of $12,000 per school, the company said.

College Card Agreements Are Not Fully Transparent

Comprehensive information about the terms of agreements between college card providers and schools was not available. Neither Education nor CFPB collects all college card contracts.[52] Some providers with which we spoke noted that they consider the contracts with schools to be proprietary or confidential, but in some cases the card issuers provided us with "template," or generic, contracts that omitted the terms specific to an individual school. Among the nine schools we reviewed, five provided us with copies of their contracts.

According to Education staff, the agency currently has the authority to require schools to provide it with card contracts, although to date Education has not issued a broad request for such contracts. However, Education staff said it is uncertain whether the agency has the authority to publicly release any contracts it might collect. In addition, it is unclear whether Education has the authority to request schools' contracts in cases where the card provider does not administer financial aid payments, which is the case at three of the large schools included in our review, as well as at many other schools with college card agreements.[53] Education staff said the agency also lacks authority to request additional information on actual college card costs incurred by students, which could be beneficial to both students and regulators. As noted earlier, Education currently encourages schools to disclose this information, but none of the nine schools included in our review provided this information to students. Similarly, in December 2013, CFPB issued an announcement calling for voluntary public disclosure by financial institutions of their college card agreements and other products marketed to students. The agency noted that students and their families should know if schools have a financial incentive to encourage students to use a specific account or card product.[54]

In prior reports, we have cited the value of transparency in such areas as improving program outcomes and strengthening oversight.[55] NACUBO's best practices recommendations call for greater transparency of college card agreements, stating that schools should publicly disclose the terms of any agreements with third parties issuing college cards to students. Some members of Congress also have cited the need for disclosure of college card contracts, saying, among other things, that transparency is needed to ensure that terms are fair and reasonable for students and the agreements are free from conflicts of interest or improper incentives.

Disclosure is required for agreements for another college-related financial product—affinity credit cards—and for student loans and lenders. Affinity credit cards typically bear the name or logo of the school or organization and, in return, the card provider pays a portion of the proceeds of the credit card back to the organization. The Credit CARD Act, together with implementing regulations, establishes requirements for disclosure to federal authorities of the contracts between these card providers and school-related entities, plus other key information, such as payments from providers.[56] Under the act, the Federal Reserve (initially) and CFPB (most recently) have produced reports that summarize the disclosure information and make it readily accessible. CFPB maintains a public database containing the affinity credit card agreements.[57]

For student loans, disclosure requirements were enacted in 2008 after lenders were found to be improperly offering schools inducements to be placed on "preferred lender" lists. To help ensure that schools list lenders that offer the best terms and conditions for students, schools that maintain a list of preferred lenders must disclose the criteria used to select the lenders and the loan terms and conditions, as well as notify students that they need not borrow from a lender on the list.[58] Similar disclosure of college card agreements could allow interested parties to review contract provisions and determine whether the agreements pose any concerns related to incentives or conflicts of interest.

Federal Agencies Have been Reviewing and Considering Further Regulation of College Cards

Education has been considering further regulation to address concerns about college cards. After holding public hearings in 2012 and 2013, Education announced in November 2013 that it was forming a committee to develop proposed regulations on a variety of federal student aid issues, including college cards. The committee is scheduled to begin work in February 2014.

CFPB issued a Request for Information in February 2013 for topics including the structure of college card agreements, the types of financial products and services offered to students, and students' experiences using these cards. CFPB received 162 comments from card providers, schools, advocacy groups, students, and others. In September 2013, CFPB hosted a forum on college cards, at which it presented initial findings from its information request and stakeholders presented their views on college cards. At the forum, the agency said continuing areas of interest included how schools can use their bargaining power to negotiate card terms that provide better deals for students than products available to the general public; how students can be better equipped to shop for services; obstacles schools face when seeking to adopt best practices on disclosure of card arrangements; and whether schools have established codes of conduct for employees who negotiate card agreements, such as those required for school employees who select preferred student lenders. CFPB staff told us they have no specific schedule or outcome planned for their college card work, including whether they will propose any regulations.

CONCLUSION

College cards may confer benefits to schools and students, but they may not be the best option for all students. Financial markets function best when consumers are fully informed about financial products and how to choose among them, and NACUBO has recommended that schools present students with information about their college cards in a neutral fashion. However, the information presented at some schools appears biased toward encouraging students to choose the college card over other options, and Education's guidance does not address the responsibility of schools to provide objective and neutral information to students about their financial aid payment options. As a result, some students may not be getting information that enables them to adequately assess whether a college card best meets their individual needs and preferences and is the most cost-effective choice among all options for conducting financial transactions and receiving student aid.

On another key issue–access to funds–Education's regulations require that college card providers offer "convenient access" to ATMs or a bank branch office where students can withdraw federal student aid without incurring cost, but the agency has not specified what constitutes this level of access. Because of the concerns about access to fee-free ATMs at schools with college cards, Education staff have acknowledged that further specifying convenient access may be beneficial. As part of its recently announced process for developing regulations on a range of federal student aid topics, including college cards, Education could consider more specific direction on what constitutes convenient access— possibly including objective measures—which could resolve ambiguity and help ensure that students at all schools with college cards would be able to readily access student aid funds at no cost.

Although millions of students attend institutions that offer college cards, comprehensive information is unavailable on the prevalence of agreements between schools and card providers, the terms of those agreements, and the experience of students in using college cards. As a result, it is difficult for policymakers and regulators to fully understand and effectively monitor the growing college card market. With the Credit CARD Act, Congress required greater transparency for college affinity credit cards, but not for college debit and prepaid cards, which were less prevalent at the time. Requiring disclosure of college debit and prepaid card agreements and related information, as well as making that information easily available, would provide greater transparency about the financial relationships between schools and card providers, and could help students, policymakers, and regulators identify potential concerns about these arrangements.

MATTER FOR CONGRESSIONAL CONSIDERATION

To help ensure a comprehensive understanding of the agreements between colleges and debit and prepaid card providers, Congress should consider requiring that providers file these agreements with CFPB for public review, and provide other relevant information, such as payments between schools and the providers and fees charged to students, and that Education provide reasonably prominent notice of the availability of such information.

RECOMMENDATIONS FOR EXECUTIVE ACTION

To help ensure that students can make an objective choice about whether to use a college card selected by their schools and have free and convenient access to federal student aid funds, the Secretary of Education should take the following actions:

- In consultation with CFPB, develop requirements that schools and college card providers present students with objective and neutral information on their options for receiving federal student aid payments.
- Provide a specific definition for what constitutes convenient access to ATMs or branch offices of debit and prepaid card providers where students will not incur costs in making cash withdrawals of federal student aid.

AGENCY COMMENTS

We provided a draft of this report to the Department of Education, the Bureau of Consumer Financial Protection, and the Federal Deposit Insurance Corporation. Education and CFPB provided written comments. In its written comments, Education concurred with our recommendations to the agency. Education reiterated that, as part of its upcoming process to develop proposed regulations for federal student aid programs, it is convening a committee that will discuss, among other things, the meaning of "convenient access" and potential requirements for schools and card providers to present students with information on federal student aid payment options. In its written comments, CFPB concurred with our Matter for Congressional Consideration, noting that the failure to disclose the nature of college card agreements raises potential consumer protection risks. CFPB also said that it will continue to monitor the college card market closely and take action as appropriate to ensure the law is being followed. Education, CFPB, and FDIC provided technical comments that were incorporated, as appropriate. We also provided selected relevant portions of the draft to other federal agencies mentioned in the report, as well as Higher One, and incorporated their technical comments as appropriate.

Sincerely yours,

Alicia Puente Cackley
Director, Financial Markets and Community Investment

Melissa Emrey-Arras
Director, Education, Workforce, and Income Security

APPENDIX I. OBJECTIVES, SCOPE, AND METHODOLOGY

This report examines (1) functions of college cards and the characteristics of schools and card providers offering the cards, and (2) benefits and concerns regarding these cards. We focused on debit and prepaid cards provided to students through agreements between schools and banks or other financial firms.

Our review did not include other card arrangements, such as "closed loop" systems, in which cards connected to predeposited funds typically can be used for payments on-campus, or on-campus and at a limited number of near-campus merchants.

Federal Agencies, Laws, and Regulations

We reviewed relevant federal laws and regulations, as well as documentation and guidance from federal agencies including the Department of Education (Education), the Bureau of Consumer Financial Protection (CFPB), the Federal Deposit Insurance Corporation (FDIC), and the Board of Governors of the Federal Reserve System (Federal Reserve). We interviewed staff from these agencies on topics that included their monitoring of college card activity and recent regulatory actions and initiatives. We reviewed public comments related to college cards that Education received during recent hearings held as part of a rulemaking process, and that CFPB received through a public Request for Information. We also reviewed debit card complaints submitted to Education and information on an FDIC enforcement action involving a college card provider.

We attended, and reviewed material provided at, a CFPB forum on financial products marketed to college students. In addition, we reviewed documentation from, and interviewed staff of, other federal programs that distribute benefits electronically on cards—the Departments of Labor, Agriculture, Health and Human Services, and the Treasury.

Data Analysis

To characterize the extent to which colleges and universities have entered into college card agreements, and to examine the financial services available through these cards, we developed a list of schools with agreements. We created this list by reviewing available data from sources including industry reports, interviews with college card providers, and information obtained from school and provider websites.[59] Our creation and analysis of this information took place over several months leading up to and including July 2013. Although we conducted an extensive search, we may not have identified all schools with agreements.

Using data from Education's Integrated Postsecondary Education Data System (IPEDS), we analyzed the institutional and student characteristics of schools we identified as having college card agreements, and compared these characteristics with those for schools and students overall. IPEDS is a system of interrelated surveys conducted annually to gather information from each college, university, and technical or vocational institution that participates in federal student aid programs.[60] We used IPEDS data for the 2011-2012 school year, the most recent available, to report on the following school characteristics: school sector, location, enrollment, level of institution (such as 2- or 4-year), and percentage of students receiving Pell Grants. We also used the IPEDS data to report on the following student characteristics: age, race, and average amounts of financial aid received.

To link the list of schools we identified as having card agreements to corresponding school and student characteristic data in IPEDS, we first used an automated process to match school names with IPEDS institution names. Most names matched successfully, but for the relatively few cases that did not, we made the match manually. Four schools from our college card agreement list did not match with IPEDS school names through either the automated or manual process. We excluded these schools from our analysis of student characteristics.

Schools may have more than one unit or location. If IPEDS listed each of a college's locations or campuses separately, we counted each as a separate school.

However, if we identified only a specific campus within a particular college system as having a card agreement, and not other campuses in the system, we included only the specific campus.

Additionally, for schools offering online instruction, if IPEDS identified them separately, we also counted them separately in our analysis.

We assessed the reliability of the IPEDS data by reviewing documentation about the systems used to produce the data and considering our previous use of the data. Based on our assessment, we concluded that IPEDS data were sufficiently reliable for our reporting purposes.

Selection of Schools for Extended Review

To complement our data analysis, we selected nine schools with college card agreements for extended interviews and data collection. We selected this nongeneralizable sample of schools to include a mix of card types (debit and prepaid cards) and functions (such as use as identification card or for student payments).

We selected schools with larger enrollments and higher proportions of students receiving federal student loans in order to focus on schools distributing larger amounts of federal student aid. We also included a mix of program lengths (for example, 4-year and 2-year), school sectors (public, nonprofit, and for- profit), card providers, and geographic locations. We interviewed officials at each of the selected schools and reviewed key documents including, where available, contracts with college card providers, card terms and conditions, and online and paper materials provided to students.

We also interviewed student leaders at five of these schools where we could arrange meetings with students. (Table 3 summarizes the characteristics of the institutions we selected and the types of cards and card services they offer.) Our interviews covered topics including college card features, how and why schools decided to enter into card agreements, contract terms, card fees, and agreement benefits and concerns.

College Card Providers and Fees

We interviewed executives of eight banks and financial firms that were the largest providers of college cards, together accounting for about 90 percent of the college card agreements we identified. The eight companies were Higher One, Inc.; U.S. Bank; Sallie Mae, Inc.; PNC Bank; Wells Fargo Bank; Citibank; Heartland Payment Systems, Inc.; and Blackboard, Inc. We reviewed documents obtained from the providers, including samples of contracts with schools and marketing materials. We also reviewed securities filings, fee schedules, and other publicly available information for the eight providers. To compare college card fees with fees for similar banking services, we also compiled fee information for basic and student checking accounts from five large banks (which account for about 30 percent of the market for large commercial banks) and for credit unions.[61] We reviewed these providers' fees for monthly account maintenance, domestic out-of-network transactions at automated teller machines (ATM), overdraft or insufficient funds, inactivity, wire transfer, and debit transactions using personal identification numbers (PIN). We selected the five large banks based on consolidated assets as of June 30, 2013, as reported by the Federal Reserve. (The banks we selected were not among the eight largest college card providers we identified.) We obtained these banks' fee information in August and September 2013 from information available on providers' websites, and when such information was not sufficient, by calling the provider's customer service line. We designated a bank's checking accounts as basic if they provided standard services such as check-writing, debit cards, and access to a bank branch. For credit union fee information, we reviewed fees reported in the Credit Union National Association's 2013-2014 Fees Report.

Industry Groups, Consumer Associations, and Other Sources

We also obtained information from other relevant parties. This included interviews with representatives from industry groups, including the American Bankers Association, the Consumer Bankers Association, and the Credit Union National Association; consumer advocacy organizations, including the National Consumer Law Center and the U.S. Public Interest Research Group; higher education associations, including the American Student Government Association, National Association of Campus Card Users, and National Association of College and University Business Officers; two schools that had canceled their college card programs (in addition to the nine schools selected for extended review); and four financial services providers, including Visa and MasterCard, that submitted public comments to CFPB regarding college cards (in addition to the eight largest providers). We reviewed documents, reports, and other information from these groups, as available.

Table 3. Institutions Selected for Extended Review, by Card Type and Services Offered

School sector and program length	Enrollment and location	Type of card		Services offered		
		Debit	Prepaid	Provider-issued card serves as student ID	School-issued student ID linked to checking	Payment of financial aid and other funds
Public 4-year	46,000 students East	X			X	
Public 4-year	15,000 students West	X				X
Public 4-year	31,000 students East	X			X	
Public 2-year	18,000 students Midwest	X			X	
Public 2-year	24,000 students Midwest	X		X	X	
Public 2-year	25,000 students West		X		X	
Private, nonprofit 4-year	74,000 students East	X			X	
Private, nonprofit 4-year	5,000 students East		X		X	
Private, for-profit 4-year	23,000 students West	X			X	

Sources: U.S. Department of Education, school officials.

We conducted this performance audit from November 2012 to February 2014 in accordance with generally accepted government auditing standards. Those standards require that we plan and perform the audit to obtain sufficient, appropriate evidence to provide a reasonable basis for our findings and conclusions based on our audit objectives.

We believe that the evidence obtained provides a reasonable basis for our findings and conclusions based on our audit objectives.

Appendix II. Comparison of Student Payments by College Cards with Other Federal Benefits Distributed by Prepaid or Electronic Benefit Cards

We reviewed several federal programs that use prepaid or electronic benefit cards to provide payments to beneficiaries (see table 4).

Although there are some similarities, these card programs generally differ from the debit and prepaid cards that some U.S. colleges and universities use to pay financial aid and other funds, which can include federal student aid funds.

Key points of comparison include:

- **Administrative structure.** The other federal programs we reviewed that use prepaid and electronic cards, some of which are run through partnerships with state governments, generally distribute aid directly to beneficiaries on prepaid and electronic benefit cards that are provided through centrally managed agreements between the federal or state governments and card providers. In contrast, federal student aid is channeled through individual schools, and these schools negotiate individual agreements with card providers.
- **Scale.** Schools with college card programs have student populations ranging from less than 1,000 to more than 100,000 students. However, other federal programs can be much larger. For example, the Department of Agriculture's Supplemental Nutrition Assistance Program (SNAP), formerly known as the Food Stamp Program, had more than 46 million participants in 2012.
- **Choice of how to receive benefits.** The Department of Education (Education) prohibits schools from requiring that students use college

cards, and funds can be paid to students by paper check; electronic transfer of funds, such as to a college card or direct deposit to an existing account; or in cash. The Department of the Treasury provides Social Security beneficiaries with a choice of receiving benefits by direct deposit or on a prepaid card, though generally not by paper check. For other federal programs, like the Department of Health and Human Services' Temporary Assistance for Needy Families program, electronic benefit transfer (EBT) cards are the only way beneficiaries can obtain their benefits in most states.

- **Card limitations.** Education requires that the federal student aid funds students receive on college cards be convertible to cash that can be used for any purpose. The Department of Labor (Labor) has similar requirements for funds provided through Unemployment Insurance benefit cards. However, other federal programs may limit where and for what items benefit cards can be used. For example, SNAP limits EBT card purchases to eligible food items from approved retailers.
- **Card fees.** Similar to Education, other federal agencies we reviewed place some limits on card user fees. Each of the programs described below requires that card users have at least one opportunity to obtain benefits without a fee. SNAP prohibits all card user fees, although states may charge a fee for replacement cards.

Among the federal programs we reviewed, the one most similar to college cards was Labor's electronic distribution of Unemployment Insurance benefits.

In both cases, beneficiaries have no limits on purchases using the card and generally have a choice in how they receive their benefits. While neither Labor nor Education negotiates contracts with card providers, both agencies impose requirements aimed at ensuring that agreements have protections for beneficiaries.

For example, both require that beneficiaries have an opportunity to access their full benefit without incurring a fee. Labor staff told us they have been developing new guidance that will likely encourage states to negotiate card agreements that minimize fees and offer beneficiaries a choice in how they receive benefits. They said they may issue the guidance early in 2014.

Table 4. Description of Selected Federal Program Benefits Issued on Prepaid or EBT Cards

Agency/program	Administrative structure and benefit options	Card usage and limitations	Card fees
Department of Agriculture • Supplemental Nutrition Assistance Program (SNAP) • Special Supplemental Nutrition Program for Women, Infants, and Children (WIC)	SNAP and WIC provide nutrition assistance to low-income individuals and families, and to pregnant and postpartum women, infants, and children, respectively. All states issue SNAP benefits solely through EBT cards, and six states currently issue WIC benefits by EBT statewide. Each state selects its own EBT card provider. However, the Department of Agriculture reviews states' requests for proposals to ensure contracts meet requirements and are awarded through competitive processes.	SNAP EBT cards can be used only to buy eligible food items from approved retailers, and WIC EBT card purchases are limited to designated packages of food. SNAP and WIC benefits cannot be accessed through automated teller machines (ATM).[a]	Federal law prohibits card fees for beneficiaries, except for a replacement card fee charged by some states.
Department of Health and Human Services[b] Temporary Assistance for Needy Families (TANF)	TANF provides cash assistance to low-income families. Each state is responsible for administering its own payment methods and	TANF EBT cards can be used to make purchases at retailers or withdraw cash at ATMs or banks, but federal and state rules restrict transactions at	Recipients must have access to benefits with minimal fees or charges, including an opportunity to access benefits with no fee or charges.

Table 4. (Continued)

Agency/program	Administrative structure and benefit options	Card usage and limitations	Card fees
	selecting an EBT card provider, if it chooses. Although some states allow recipients to choose among payment methods (EBT card, paper check), EBT cards are the only option in the majority of states.	certain locations, such as liquor stores and casinos.[c]	
Department of the Treasury Direct Express card for Social Security, Supplemental Security Income, and other federal benefit programs	Federal regulations require federal benefit payments to be made electronically. Beneficiaries can choose between direct deposit into personal bank accounts or the Direct Express prepaid card issued by Comerica Bank.	Direct Express cards can be used to make purchases and get cash from ATMs or bank locations nationwide that accept MasterCard. No restrictions on purchases.	No monthly account fees or fees on domestic purchases (including cash back with purchases) or bank withdrawals. Customers receive one free withdrawal from a network ATM with each benefit deposit onto the card, but are charged $0.90 for each additional withdrawal.
Department of Labor Unemployment Insurance	Unemployment Insurance benefits are provided to eligible workers who become unemployed through no fault of their own. Benefits are	Cards can be used to make purchases and get cash from ATMs or bank locations. No restrictions on purchases.	Beneficiaries must have at least one opportunity to access the full amount of the weekly or biweekly benefit for free. Other fees are deter-

Agency/program	Administrative structure and benefit options	Card usage and limitations	Card fees
	administered by individual states, which determine their distribution methods. More than 40 states currently issue benefits on cards.		mined through negotiations between individual states and card providers. In general, states and card providers allow unlimited free in-network ATM withdrawals, with limited free out-of-network ATM withdrawals. ATM fees range from \$0.40 to \$2.50 depending on the state and whether the ATM is in the provider's network.

Source: GAO analysis of agency interviews and documents.

[a] For additional information on SNAP EBT cards, see GAO, *Supplemental Nutrition Assistance Program: Payment Errors and Trafficking Have Declined, but Challenges Remain*, GAO-10-956T (Washington, D.C.: July 28, 2010).

[b] The Department of Health and Human Services also administers the Child Care Development Fund program. Most payments for this program are made by states directly to child care providers. However, two states (Kansas and Utah) currently distribute payments to parents using EBT cards. In these cases, parents use the EBT cards to pay their child care providers directly. Because the bulk of states do not have this EBT card arrangement, we omit the program from the table.

[c] Federal law prohibits TANF assistance from being accessed via any EBT transaction in liquor stores, casinos or gaming establishments, and any establishment which provides adult-oriented entertainment in which performers disrobe or perform in an unclothed state for entertainment. Middle Class Tax Relief and Job Creation Act of 2012, Pub. L. No. 112–96, § 4004, 126 Stat. 156, 197–198 (codified at 42 U.S.C. § 608(a)(12)). For more information, see GAO, *TANF Electronic Benefit Cards: Some States Are Restricting Certain TANF Transactions, but Challenges Remain*, GAO-12-535 (Washington, D.C.: July 20, 2012).

Appendix III. Comparison of College Card Fees among Providers, Other Institutions, and Account Types

To examine the costs of college card accounts, we obtained publicly available fee information for college card providers on selected items or transactions as of August and September 2013. We also obtained publicly available fee information for products similar to college cards–basic and student checking accounts–offered by other financial institutions.

College Cards

Table 5. Fees for College Cards, by College Card Provider and Type, as of August-September 2013

	Card type	Monthly maintenance fee	ATM out-of-network fee (domestic)[a]	Insufficient funds/ overdraft fee	Wire transfer fee[b]	Monthly inactivity fee	PIN-based debit transaction fee
Higher One: OneAccount	Debit	$0[c]	$2.50	$29[d]	$25 outgoing	$0	$0.50
Higher One: OneAccount Edge	Debit	$4.95	$0	$0	Not applicable[e]	$0	$0
Higher One: OneAccount Premier	Debit	$5.95[f]	$2.50[g]	$29[d]	$25 outgoing	$0	$0
U.S. Bank	Debit[h]	$0	$2.50	$36[i]	$20 incoming, $30 outgoing	$0	$0
	Prepaid	$0	$2	Not applicable	$0	$2 (after 9 months of inactivity)	$0

	Card type	Monthly maintenance fee	ATM out-of-network fee (domestic)[a]	Insufficient funds/ overdraft fee	Wire transfer fee[b]	Monthly inactivity fee	PIN-based debit transaction fee
Blackboard	Prepaid	$0	$2.50	Not applicable	Not applicable	$3.50 (after 24 months of inactivity)	$0
Heartland Payment Systems	Prepaid	$0	$2	Not applicable	$0	$5 (after 24 months of inactivity)	$0
PNC	Prepaid	$5	$2.50	$0	$15 incoming, $25 outgoing	$0	$0
	Debit	$0[j]	$2.50	$36[k]	$15 incoming, $25 outgoing[l]	$15 (after 6 months of inactivity)	$0
Wells Fargo	Debit	$0	$2.50	$0[m]	$15 incoming, $30 outgoing	$0	$0
Sallie Mae[n]	Prepaid	$4.95[o]	$2.50	$0	Not applicable[p]	Not listed	Not listed
Citibank	Prepaid	$0	$3	Not applicable	Not listed	$3 (after 12 months of inactivity)[q]	$0.50[r]

Source: GAO analysis of publically available fee schedules and provider information.

Note: Fees shown as "Not applicable" were listed as such in account materials or as described by providers.

[a] Students also may incur fees from the ATM owner. All out-of-network ATM fees are for domestic withdrawals.

[b] The fees are for domestic wire transfers. Some providers also offer alternative, potentially less expensive options for transferring money to another account, such as depositing paper checks.

[c] Nonstudent accountholders are charged $3.95, which is waived with $100 in direct deposit per month.

[d] Higher One will not authorize ATM withdrawals or everyday one-time or recurring debit card purchases when the accountholder does not have sufficient funds in the account to cover the withdrawal or purchase. Student would be charged $29 for first item and $38 for any subsequent item. Higher One does not provide overdraft protection for its checking accounts.

[e] OneAccount Edge accountholders cannot perform wire transfers.

[f] The fee is waived with $300 in direct deposits each month.

[g] OneAccount Premier accountholders receive one monthly non-Higher One ATM withdrawal fee reimbursement.

[h] According to U.S. Bank, its debit cards can be attached to any one of U.S. Bank's checking accounts, each with different options and fees. Fees shown here apply to the U.S Bank Student Checking account, which the bank said is the most popular account chosen by students.

[i] No fee is charged for items of $5 or less. A $36 fee is charged for items more than $5.

[j] No monthly service charge if the customer provides proof of active enrollment in qualifying educational institution (expires 6 years after account is enrolled in student banking program).

[k] According to PNC, overdraft fees are waived for the first overdraft.

[l] Customers in the Student Banking program enrolled at a designated PNC Alliance or Access school continue to receive one free domestic or international incoming wire transfer per statement period.

[m] If an accountholder adds Debit Card Overdraft Service and an ATM or everyday debit card transaction overdraws the account, a $35 fee will be charged per item. If the accountholder does not add the service, the ATM or everyday debit card transaction will be declined and no overdraft fee will be charged.

[n] Higher One acquired Sallie Mae's student card operations in 2013.

[o] The charge is waived in any monthly billing cycle when the customer receives a payment, posts 15 qualifying purchase transactions, or loads at least $1,000 on the card.

[p] Sallie Mae's prepaid card did not accept wired funds.

[q] Following a 12-month grace period; an inactive account is defined as any account that has not received a payment or completed a withdrawal transaction within 90 days.

[r] The first PIN transaction fee is waived per each deposit to the card account.

Other Financial Institutions

Table 6. Fees for Other Banking Products Available to Students, by Provider and Type, as of August-September 2013

	Account type	Monthly maintenance fee	ATM out-of-network fee (domestic)	Insufficient funds/ overdraft fee	Domestic wire transfer fee	Inactivity fee	PIN-based debit transaction fee
JP Morgan Chase	Basic	$12[a]	$2	$34	$15 incoming, $30 outgoing[b]	$0	$0
	Student[c]	$6[d]	$2	$34	$15 incoming, $30 outgoing[e]	$0	$0
Bank of America	Basic	$12[f]	$2	$35[g]	$12 incoming, $25 outgoing	$0	$0
	Student	$0[h]	$2	$35[g]	$12 incoming, $25 outgoing	$0	$0
Capital One Bank	Basic	$8.95[i]	$2	$35	$15 incoming, $25 outgoing	$0	$0
	Student	$0	$2	$35	$15 incoming, $25 outgoing	$0	$0
TD Bank	Basic	$5.99[j]	$2.50	$35	$15 incoming, $25 outgoing	$0	$0
	Student	$0	$2.50	$0[k]	$15 incoming, $25 outgoing	$0	$0
	Basic	$10[l]	$2.50	$0[m]	$15 incoming, $24 outgoing	$0	$0
BB&T	Student	$0	$2.50[n]	$0[m]	$15 incoming, $24 outgoing	$0	$0

Table 6. (Continued)

	Account type	Monthly maintenance fee	ATM out-of-network fee (domestic)	Insufficient funds/ overdraft fee	Domestic wire transfer fee	Inactivity fee	PIN-based debit transaction fee
Credit unions (median fees)[o]		$0	$1	$25 insufficient funds fee, $4 overdraft fee	$15 outgoing, $10 incoming[p]	Not available	$0
Community banks				Comprehensive information not available			

Source: GAO analysis of publically available fee schedules and provider information.

[a] The fee is $10 in California, Oregon, and Washington. The monthly service charge can be avoided if the customer does any one of the following each monthly statement period: makes direct deposits totaling $500 or more into the account monthly; maintains $1,500 minimum daily balance; maintains average daily balance of $5,000 or more in any combination of qualifying linked deposits or investments; or pays $25 or more in qualifying checking-related services or fees.

[b] The domestic outgoing charge is $25 if a transfer is made through chase.com.

[c] The account is for college students age 17-24 when proof of student status is provided.

[d] No monthly maintenance fee is charged if the customer has done one of the following: enrolled in college (up to 5 years); made a direct deposit to the account monthly; or maintained a $5,000 monthly average daily balance.

[e] The domestic outgoing charge is $25 if the transfer is made through chase.com.

[f] The fee is waived if the customer does one of the following each statement period: makes at least one direct deposit of $250, or maintains an average daily balance of $1,500 or more.

[g] Bank of America will not authorize ATM withdrawals or everyday debit card purchases when the customer does not have sufficient funds in the account. A fee is assessed for scheduled payments and checks.

[h] A $12 monthly maintenance fee is charged if the accountholder is not enrolled in school or under age 23.

[i] The fee is waived with a $300 minimum daily balance or single monthly direct deposit of $250 or more.

[j] The fee is $4.95 when customer chooses online statements only.

[k] If the accountholder adds overdraft service, a $35 fee is charged per ATM or debit card transaction. If the accountholder does not add this service, the ATM or everyday debit card transaction will be declined and no overdraft fee charged.

[l] The fee is waived with one automated direct deposit of $100 or greater per statement period; $1,500 average checking balance per statement period; or $6,000 in combined deposit or retail outstanding loan balances.

[m] Accountholders can opt in to overdraft protection, which allows the bank to authorize transactions when the account has insufficient funds; they will be charged a fee. If accountholder does not opt in, the transaction will be declined and a fee assessed.

[n] Student banking accountholders receive four no-fee non-BB&T transactions per statement period.

[o] Based on survey responses from 1,000 credit unions. Median fee amounts are based on credit unions that charged a particular fee. When the majority of credit unions did not charge a specific fee, the median amount was reported as $0. See Credit Union National Association, Fees Report 2013- 2014, conducted from November 2012 through February 2013.

[p] Data from Credit Union National Association 2010-2011 survey, because this data element was not included in the 2013-2014 survey.

APPENDIX IV. FEDERAL PROVISIONS ADDRESSING DEBIT AND PREPAID CARDS

A number of federal laws and regulations can apply to debit and prepaid cards. With the exception of education-specific items, these provisions apply generally to such cards, and do not specifically address college debit and prepaid cards. In general, debit cards have greater consumer protections than prepaid cards. Table 7 shows summaries of key provisions.

Table 7. Federal Provisions Addressing Debit and Prepaid Cards

Law/regulation	Debit cards	Prepaid cards[a]
Electronic Fund Transfer Act 15 U.S.C. §§ 1693-1693r Regulation E	• Cardholder liability limited to $50 if cardholder notifies issuing financial institution within 2 business days after	• Regulation E generally does not apply, but Bureau of Consumer Financial Protection (CFPB) has issued an advance notice of

Table 7. (Continued)

Law/regulation	Debit cards	Prepaid cards[a]
12 C.F.R. Part 1005	discovering the loss or theft of an access device. Notification after 2 business days may result in loss of up to $500 (or more, in certain circumstances). • Financial institutions must disclose fees associated with debit card and must issue statement for each monthly cycle in which a transaction occurred and at least quarterly if no transaction occurred. • Financial institutions must provide 21-day notice before altering fee schedule or liability limits for unauthorized transactions. • Cardholders must provide their financial institutions with written permission to allow institution to charge overdraft fee for one-time debit card or ATM transaction use while balance is negative ("opt in").	proposed rulemaking as it considers whether to extend the regulation's protections to prepaid cards. • Cardholder liability not limited under federal law, although liability may be limited by contract. • No disclosure or periodic statement requirements under federal law. • No requirement that card issuers provide notice of fee changes. Prepaid cards also may have more fee types than debit cards. • Generally, cardholder cannot spend more than card's loaded value. • Credit CARD Act restrictions[b] on dormancy fees, service fees, or expiration dates apply only to gift cards, not to cards used more generally as replacements for checking or deposit accounts.
Family Educational Rights and Privacy Act (FERPA) 20 U.S.C. § 1232g 34 CFR Part 99	• Generally, institutions of postsecondary education must have written permission from students to release personally identifiable information from student's education record. However, FERPA allows disclosure of student records without prior consent to "school officials"–who can be outside parties contracted by the schools, such as debit card	Loading of card with personally identifiable information before student consents to the relationship is a violation of FERPA.

Law/regulation	Debit cards	Prepaid cards[a]
	providers–with a legitimate educational interest, and to appropriate parties in connection with financial aid. • Schools may disclose without consent directory information," such as a student's name, address, and date of birth. • Outside parties receiving student information must give the information the same protection as schools and can use it only for intended purpose. • FERPA does not apply until student begins attending the school.	
Federal deposit insurance	Underlying checking or deposit accounts to which debit cards are tied carry up to $250,000 in mandatory Federal Deposit Insurance Corporation (FDIC) insurance.	• Funds linked to prepaid card may or may not be insured. Cardholders may not be covered by deposit insurance if FDIC requirements for "pass-through" insurance not met.[c] • Card issuers may choose whether to cover the product with FDIC insurance. Others may opt for coverage through state money transmitter licenses, which require a surety bond.
Expedited Funds Availability Act 12 U.S.C. §§ 4001-4010 Regulation CC 12 CFR Part 229	Electronic payments must be made available on first business day following banking day of deposit ("next-day availability"). Transaction accountholders must receive disclosures on when funds will be available.	Generally, prepaid cards not subject to Regulation CC, but the provision could apply, depending on card features.
Regulation II (debit card interchange fees and routing) 12 C.F.R. Part 235	• Debit cards are subject to regulatory standards for assessing whether interchange fees received by debit card issuer for	Certain prepaid cards are exempt from interchange fee limitations. If prepaid card is only means of accessing underlying funds

Table 7. (Continued)

Law/regulation	Debit cards	Prepaid cards[a]
	electronic debit transaction are reasonable and proportional to the costs incurred by issuer for the transaction. • Interchange fee standards do not apply to interchange fees charged or received by debit card issuer that has total assets of less than $10 billion (with affiliates) and holds the account being debited.	(except when all remaining funds are provided to cardholder in single transaction), interchange fee standards do not apply.
Law/regulation	**Debit cards and Prepaid cards**	
Higher Education Act of 1965, as amended, Title IV 20 U.S.C. §§ 1070-1099d and 42 U.S.C. §§ 2751-2756b 34 C.F.R. § 668.164	• Regulations implementing Title IV permit payment of funds to student or parent bank account, defined as an account insured by FDIC or the National Credit Union Share Insurance Fund. The account may be one that "underlies a stored-value card or other transaction device." • When a school opens a bank account on behalf of a student or assists a student in opening a bank account, the school must, among other things: obtain written consent from the student to open the account; inform the student of the terms of account prior to opening; ensure the student does not incur costs in opening account or receiving a debit or ATM card; and ensure the student has "convenient access" to ATM or branch of the bank. • When a school opens a bank account for a student, regulations prohibit the school from subsequently converting the account or card to a credit card or credit instrument. • Credit balances that remain after the school applies Title IV funds to pay tuition, fees, and room and board must be paid to the student as soon as possible but (1) no later than 14 days after balance occurred if the balance occurred after first day of class; or (2) no later than 14 days after first day of class of a payment period if balance occurred on or before first day of class of payment period.	

Law/regulation	Debit cards and Prepaid cards
Federal Trade Commission Act, Sec. 5 15 U.S.C. § 45 Consumer Financial Protection Act of 2010 (CFPB authority regarding unfair, deceptive, or abusive acts or practices) 12 U.S.C. § 5531	• Section 5 of Federal Trade Commission Act (FTC Act) prohibits unfair or deceptive acts or practices. • The Federal Trade Commission (FTC) has FTC Act jurisdiction over financial products and services offered by entities other than banks, thrifts, federal credit unions, certain nonprofit organizations, and those specifically exempt from FTC jurisdiction. • The Office of the Comptroller of the Currency, Board of Governors of the Federal Reserve System, and FDIC have FTC Act jurisdiction for financial institutions they regulate. • The Dodd-Frank Wall Street Reform and Consumer Protection Act, which created CFPB, gives the agency enforcement authority over unfair, deceptive, or abusive acts or practices by covered persons or service providers.[d] • An act or practice may be unfair if it causes, or is likely to cause, "substantial injury" to consumers; is not reasonably avoidable; and any injury is not outweighed by benefits to consumers or competition. • Using FTC standard for deception, CFPB may find acts or practices deceptive if the representation, act, or practice is material and misleads or is likely to mislead a consumer, and the consumer's interpretation is reasonable under the circumstances. • CFPB may declare an act or practice "abusive" if (i) it "materially interferes" with a consumer's ability to understand terms of a financial product or (ii) if it takes unreasonable advantage of the consumer's (a) lack of understanding of the material risks, costs, or conditions of a product, (b) a consumer's inability to protect his/herself in selecting or using the financial product, or (c) consumer's reasonable reliance on a person to act in the interests of the consumer.
Regulation P (privacy provisions of Gramm-Leach-Bliley Act) 12 C.F.R. Part 1016	• Initial disclosure of a privacy policy must be made when customer relationship for purchase of financial product or service is established with an institution. • Financial institutions also must annually explain their data-sharing process and provide cardholders with an opportunity to opt out of certain information-sharing arrangements. • An institution of higher education that complies with FERPA and also is a financial institution subject to FTC's enforcement jurisdiction is deemed to be in compliance with Regulation P.

Source: GAO review of laws and regulations.

[a] We use “prepaid card” to mean general-purpose reloadable cards.

[b] Credit Card Accountability Responsibility and Disclosure Act of 2009, Pub. L. No. 111-24, § 401, 123 Stat. 1734, 1751-1754.

[c] According to FDIC, funds placed on a prepaid card may or may not be covered by deposit insurance in the event of a bank failure, depending on how the account where the funds are held is set up and whether the bank or the card issuer’s records at the time of the bank closing identify each cardholder’s ownership interest. See www.fdic.gov/consumers/consumer/news/cnsum12/paymentcards.html.

[d] Pub. L. No. 111-203, § 1031(a), 124 Stat. 1376, 2005 (2010).

End Notes

[1] For this report, we define federal student aid programs as financial aid programs authorized under Title IV of the Higher Education Act of 1965, as amended (codified at 20 U.S.C. §§ 1070-1099d and 42 U.S.C. §§ 2751-2756b). These programs include the Pell Grant Program and the William D. Ford Federal Direct Loan Program.

[2] Nonprofit refers to not-for-profit colleges. Private colleges also can be for-profit, so we distinguish between nonprofit and for-profit.

[3] Debit and prepaid cards are distinct from credit cards in that debit and prepaid cards do not provide a line of credit. The Credit Card Accountability Responsibility and Disclosure Act of 2009 (Credit CARD Act), Pub. L. No. 111-24, 123 Stat. 1734, mandated that GAO conduct a separate review of college affinity credit cards—credit cards issued in conjunction with a school or school-related organization. § 305(b), 123 Stat. at 1750-51. That report is scheduled to be issued in late February 2014.

[4] In this report, we use prepaid card to refer to general-purpose reloadable cards.

[5] For this report, we focus on the use of college cards to pay financial aid to students. A school may make student payments in other situations, including when (1) other payments are credited to a student's account, such as veterans educational benefits, education savings plans, or payments by other parties; or (2) a school's charges are reduced due to changes in a student's course load, housing, or meal plan, according to the National Association of College and University Business Officers.

[6] Schools are not required to follow federal rules for making payments involving nonfederal funds. However, according to the National Association of College and University Business Officers, schools generally do so—because they must follow federal rules for federal money and because funds from multiple sources may collect in a student account.

[7] See Department of Education, Office of Postsecondary Education, *Disbursing or Delivering Title IV Funds Through a Contractor*, "Dear Colleague" Letter GEN-12-08 (Apr. 26, 2012).

[8] 15 U.S.C. § 45.

[9] See 12 C.F.R. § 1005.4, § 1005.6. CFPB has issued an advance notice of proposed rulemaking as it considers extending Regulation E protections to prepaid cards. See Electronic Fund Transfers (Regulation E), 77 Fed. Reg. 30923 (May 24, 2012). According to CFPB staff, the rulemaking is expected to conclude in mid-2014.

[10] CFPB's enforcement authority is limited; it has primary enforcement authority for consumer financial protection laws against large banks and certain nondepository entities, but not against smaller banks, which are supervised by the federal banking agencies.

[11] We used IPEDS data to calculate the approximate number of colleges and universities that participated in federal student aid programs in the 2011-2012 school year.

[12] In addition to the college cards we describe here, some schools also operate "closed loop" systems, in which cards connected to predeposited funds typically can be used for payments on campus only, or on-campus and at a limited number of near-campus merchants. This kind of card is not the subject of this report.

[13] For our analysis, we relied upon the schools' descriptions of services provided under their card agreements, which we obtained largely from information provided to students on the schools' websites. We did not independently verify the services represented. See appendix I for details of our methodology.

[14] Because there is no authoritative source for this information, we conducted an extensive search to identify schools with agreements. However, all schools with agreements may not have been identified through this process. We also excluded from our analysis 13 agreements for cards that use the school logo but otherwise offer no school-related services.

[15] Overall, while schools with student populations of 20,000 or more made up about 3 percent of all schools, they accounted for about 13 percent of schools that had college card agreements.

[16] For example, nonwhite students represented about 44 percent of enrollment at schools with agreements and 41 percent at schools without agreements. Similarly, students age 25 and older represented about 33 percent of students at schools with agreements and 34 percent at schools without. Schools with college card agreements had a slightly lower percentage of students receiving financial aid grants (federal, state, local, institutional, or other) than schools overall, and the average amount of aid students received was somewhat smaller as well. IPEDS data on student characteristics were not available for four schools with college card agreements, and we omitted these schools from our analysis.

[17] About 65 percent of students receive some form of financial aid. However, Education staff told us they do not have information on how many of those receiving aid receive financial aid payments in excess of a school's charges.

[18] According to CFPB, a nonbank is a company that offers consumer financial products or services, but does not have a bank, thrift, or credit union charter and does not take deposits.

[19] Interchange fees are paid by a merchant (or an "acquirer"), and charged or received by a payment card network, in order to compensate a card issuer for its involvement in an electronic debit transaction. (An acquirer is an entity that contracts with a merchant to provide settlement for the merchant's electronic debit transactions over a payment card network.) For example, see GAO, *Credit Cards: Rising Interchange Fees Have Increased Costs for Merchants, but Options for Reducing Fees Pose Challenges*, GAO-10-45 (Washington, D.C.: Nov. 19, 2009).

[20] In August 2012, Higher One acquired the assets of Campus Labs, which provides data collection, reporting, and analytics services to institutions of higher education.

[21] Although several schools cited benefits from contracting out their student payment process, some schools told us they did not want to outsource the process, either to maintain control or because they believed they already were operating efficiently.

[22] FDIC estimated that 17 percent of householders aged 15-24 were unbanked in 2011, although the percentage may be lower for college students because householders with a high school degree or some college education were less likely to be unbanked. See Federal Deposit Insurance Corporation, *2011 FDIC National Survey of Unbanked and Underbanked Households* (Washington, D.C.: September 2012).

[23] For example, some banks will not open new accounts for individuals with a history of overdrafts on prior bank accounts.

[24] According to card providers, funds are available on college cards on the same day the school transfers funds because the funds can be deposited immediately into the cardholder account. Direct deposits into another bank account take longer because the transaction must be processed through the Automated Clearing House network and the receiving bank must verify the funds. Paper checks take the longest because they must be prepared, mailed to students or picked up, and cleared by the student's bank.

[25] As we have noted, although financial education efforts by the private sector can be beneficial, they also can raise concerns about the objectivity of the information provided. See GAO, *Financial Literacy: Enhancing the Effectiveness of the Federal Government's Role*, GAO-12-636T (Washington, D.C.: Apr. 26, 2012); and *Financial Literacy: A Federal Certification Process for Providers Would Pose Challenges,* GAO-11-614 (Washington, D.C.: June 28, 2011).

[26] We reviewed fee schedules for college cards from eight providers that together accounted for about 90 percent of the market we identified—Blackboard, Citibank, Heartland, Higher One, PNC, Sallie Mae, U.S. Bank, and Wells Fargo. We compared college card fees for account maintenance, ATM transactions, overdraft, account inactivity, debit transactions using personal identification numbers (PIN), and wire transfers with fees for banking products that a student might use as alternatives to college cards. We use "student checking" to refer to checking accounts specifically intended for, or targeted at, students, but not obtained through a college card agreement. We obtained the fee information in August and September 2013.

[27] For additional information on the use of alternative financial services, see Federal Deposit Insurance Corporation, *2011 FDIC National Survey of Unbanked and Underbanked Households* (Washington, D.C.: September 2012).

[28] The Higher One fee for PIN transactions is for its basic account. Interchange fees vary based in part on whether a transaction is authenticated by PIN or signature. Under current debit rules, depending on the size of the bank involved, signature transactions can provide higher interchange revenue. For example, because Higher One contracts with a bank with less than $10 billion in assets, the company may receive higher interchange fees for signature transactions than for PIN transactions. For more information on interchange fees generally, see GAO-10-45.

[29] According to FDIC staff, there may be disadvantages for signature transactions as well. For example, a signature transaction may be less secure from fraud than a PIN-based transaction.

[30] Negotiated Rulemaking Committee; Public Hearings, 77 Fed. Reg. 25658, 25659 (May 1, 2012).

[31] We analyzed the comments, which were solicited by CFPB in its *Request for Information Regarding Financial Products Marketed to Students Enrolled in Institutions of Higher Education*, 78 Fed. Reg. 8114 (Feb. 5, 2013).

[32] Some card providers indicated that students may access their funds through other mechanisms that do not incur fees, such as using the card to make purchases or using the cash-back option offered by some retailers, although the latter option may incur a $0.50 PIN fee, as noted earlier.

[33] We estimated the average ATM surcharge fee in 2012 was $2.10. See GAO, *Automated Teller Machines: Some Consumer Fees Have Increased*, GAO-13-266 (Washington, D.C.: Apr. 11, 2013). Financial institutions operate ATMs as a convenience to their accountholders, who generally do not pay fees to use these ATMs. However, financial institutions assess a surcharge when a transaction is made by nonaccountholders, and independent ATM operators assess surcharges on most customers.

[34] Students at schools with only one in-network ATM on campus may have access to other in-network ATMs near the campus, particularly if it is in an urban setting.

[35] Higher One waives the $5.95 monthly service fee on its premier account if the accountholder deposits $300 or more in funds per month other than financial aid payments.

[36] 34 C.F.R. § 668.164(c)(3)(v). Education guidance specifies that the intent of these regulations is to ensure that students can make unlimited withdrawals from their on- campus ATMs without incurring a fee. While some students may want to withdraw their entire financial aid payment when it becomes available, other students may make smaller withdrawals over time.

[37] See 34 C.F.R. 668.164(c)(3)(v).

[38] See Negotiated Rulemaking Committee; Public Hearings, 77 Fed. Reg. 25658 (May 1, 2012).

[39] See Negotiated Rulemaking Committee, Negotiator Nominations and Schedule of Committee Meetings—Title IV Federal Student Aid Programs, Program Integrity and Improvement, 78 Fed. Reg. 69612 (Nov. 20, 2013).

[40] For example, one provider told us that data are aggregated in a way that does not allow them to identify the fees specifically associated with their college cards and another provider said some cardholders are not students (such as faculty).

[41] See GAO-11-614.

[42] FDIC determined that the two companies violated Section 5 of the Federal Trade Commission Act by charging student accountholders multiple insufficient funds fees from a single transaction; allowing accounts to remain in overdrawn status for long periods and allowing these insufficient funds fees to continue accruing; and collecting the fees from subsequent deposits to the students' accounts, typically funds for tuition and other college expenses.

[43] The settlement also required Higher One to not make misleading or deceptive representations or omissions in its marketing materials or disclosures and to institute a sound compliance management system.

[44] The settlement also imposed civil money penalties of $172,000 for The Bancorp Bank and required it to take certain steps to improve its compliance and risk management, and provide FDIC details related to the termination of its relationship with Higher One.

[45] The parties have been working to resolve details, and a final settlement agreement requires court approval. See Higher One Holdings, Inc., Current Report (Form 8-K), (Nov. 5, 2013).

[46] Two college card providers noted that schools sometimes have exclusivity agreements with other financial services providers that can affect the college card services—for example, one card provider said that at some large public schools, it cannot locate an ATM, or have access to students, in areas used for intercollegiate sports because another financial institution already secured that exclusive right.

[47] Based on information obtained from schools and providers, we did not identify instances of cross-marketing, in which providers used student personal information obtained from schools to market products other than their debit or prepaid cards, or to share such information with third parties for marketing purposes.

[48] An additional option for deposit to another account provides for electronic filing of documentation, but requires a 6-day hold on the account, according to the provider.

[49] See Department of Education "Dear Colleague" Letter GEN-12-08; 34 C.F.R. § 668.164(c)(3)(ii).

[50] See Bureau of Consumer Financial Protection, *Reminder: Accessing Your Scholarships and Student Loan Funds*, Sept. 5, 2013, accessed Nov. 12, 2013, http://www.consumerfinance.gov/blog/reminder-accessing-your-scholarships-and-student-loan-funds/.

[51] We did not perform an in-depth review of this college card provider's products because it did not meet our criteria for the largest card providers, described in appendix I, but our review of fees associated with that provider's college card student accounts found them not significantly different from most college card fees we describe earlier in this report.

[52] According to Education, schools must provide the department with copies of contracts they enter into with "third-party servicers," as outside vendors are known, but only upon request. Education staff told us that while the agency collects general information on third- party servicers, they do not have the ability to identify college card agreements. CFPB staff similarly told us they do not broadly collect information related to the use of the cards or the agreements between schools and issuers. CFPB can investigate (through supervision, examinations, or enforcement) a report of an unfair or abusive practice, but the review would be specific to the facts in the case. As part of an investigation, CFPB could examine specific agreements.

[53] See 34 C.F.R. § 668.25(e)(2). Education's general authority to request college card contracts from schools is limited to instances when the contract involves processing any aspect of the institution's participation in federal student aid programs.

[54] See Bureau of Consumer Financial Protection, *CFPB Calls on Financial Institutions to Publicly Disclose Campus Financial Agreements*, Dec. 17, 2013, accessed Jan. 10, 2014, http://www.consumerfinance.gov/newsroom/cfpb-calls-on-financial-institutions-to-publicly- disclose-campus-financial-agreements.

[55] For example, see GAO, *Troubled Asset Relief Program: Further Actions Needed to Enhance Assessments and Transparency of Housing Programs*, GAO-12-783 (Washington, D.C.: July 19, 2012); *Financial Stability: New Council and Research Office Should Strengthen the Accountability and Transparency of Their Decisions*, GAO-12-886 (Washington, D.C.: Sept. 11, 2012); and *Federal Reserve Bank Governance: Opportunities Exist to Broaden Director Recruitment Efforts and Increase Transparency*, GAO-12-18 (Washington, D.C.: Oct. 19, 2011).

[56] Pub. L. No. 111-24, § 305(a), 123 Stat. 1734, 1750 (codified at 15 U.S.C. § 1637(r)); 12 C.F.R. § 1026.57. College affinity credit card issuers must submit to CFPB annually, among other

things, copies of any college credit card agreements to which the card issuer was a party during the prior year, the amount of any payments the issuer made to a school or affiliated organization under the agreement during the same period, and the number of credit cards opened under the agreement during the period. 12 C.F.R. § 1026.57(d)(2). The schools must disclose publicly any marketing agreement made with a card issuer. 12 C.F.R. § 1026.57(b).

[57] See www.consumerfinance.gov/credit-cards/college-agreements. The Federal Reserve also maintains a database for the years for which it was responsible for the information. See www.federalreserve.gov/collegecreditcardagreements.

[58] 20 U.S.C. § 1094(h)(1)(C).

[59] In developing this list, we also identified a small number of agreements for "co-branded" debit cards that used the school logo but otherwise provided no services to the school. We excluded these agreements from our review.

[60] The Higher Education Act of 1965, as amended, requires institutions that participate in federal student aid programs to report data on enrollments, program completions, graduation rates, faculty and staff, finances, institutional prices, and student financial aid. See 20 U.S.C. §§ 1070-1099d, 42 U.S.C. §§ 2751-2756b, and 20 U.S.C. § 1094(a)(17).

[61] Student checking accounts here means accounts offered to college students generally, and not through a college card agreement.

INDEX

D

E

F

T

U

V

W

Y